ALPHA
Questions of Life

By the same author:
Why Jesus?
Why Christmas?
Searching Issues
A Life Worth Living
Telling Others
Challenging Lifestyle
The Heart of Revival
30 Days

ALPHA
Questions of Life

Nicky Gumbel

Alpha

First published 1993
Revised edition 1995
New edition 2001
New edition 2003
Revised edition 2007

Text cartoons by Charlie Mackesy

ISBN 9 78184 291 32 84

4 5 6 7 8 9 Print / Year 12 11 10 09

Published by
KINGSWAY COMMUNICATIONS LTD
Lottbridge Drove, Eastbourne, BN23 6NT, England.
Email: books@kingsway.co.uk
Printed in the United States of America

Contents

Foreword

This book has come at exactly the right time. It fills a gap which has existed in Christian literature for several years. On the one hand, as recent well documented figures show, the church in England has been losing members at an alarming rate, particularly among young people under the age of twenty. While it is certainly true that a number of churches are showing very encouraging signs of growth, the overall picture in the country is still one of perceived dullness, decay and, as Nicky shows in this book, disillusion generally with church life. And yet . . . on the other hand there is beyond any question a very considerable new interest in spiritual things, together with a hunger and growing hope that somewhere, somehow, there may be found a contemporary answer to the age-old question, 'What is truth?'

Questions of Life is a sympathetic, fascinating and immensely readable introduction to Jesus Christ – still the most attractive and captivating person it is possible to know. Nicky Gumbel's intelligent, well researched and informed approach ensures that the search for Truth fully engages our minds as well as our hearts.

I am very glad that all the hard work that Nicky has put into the Alpha course here, through which literally hundreds of people have been deeply affected, is now available to an even wider public. I have no hesitation in highly commending this readable and important book.

Sandy Millar
Holy Trinity Brompton

Preface

There is today a new interest in the Christian faith, and more specifically in the person of Jesus. Nearly two thousand years since his birth he has approaching two billion followers. Christians will always be fascinated by the founder of their faith and the Lord of their lives. But now, there is a resurgence of interest among non-churchgoers. Many are asking questions about Jesus. Was he merely a man or is he the Son of God? If he is, what are the implications for our everyday lives?

This book attempts to answer some of the key questions at the heart of the Christian faith. It is based on 'Alpha', a course run at Holy Trinity Brompton for non-churchgoers, those seeking to find out more about Christianity, and those who have recently come to faith in Jesus Christ. We have watched in astonishment as Alpha has spread to over 18,000 courses in over 120 countries. Thousands of men and women of all ages have come on the course full of questions about Christianity, and have found God as their Father, Jesus Christ as their Saviour and Lord and the Holy Spirit as the one who comes to live within them.

I would like to thank all the people who have read and offered constructive criticisms on the manuscripts, and Cressida Inglis-

Jones who typed the original manuscript and almost all the revisions with great speed, efficiency and patience.

Nicky Gumbel

1

Is There
More to Life Than This?

For many years I had three objections to the Christian faith. First, I thought it was boring. I went to chapel at school and found it very dull. I felt sympathy with Robert Louis Stevenson who once entered in his diary, as if recording an extraordinary phenomenon, 'I have been to Church today, and am not depressed.' In a similar vein, the American humorist, Oliver Wendell Holmes, wrote, 'I might have entered the ministry if certain clergymen I knew had not looked and acted so much like undertakers.' My impression of the Christian faith was that it was dreary and uninspiring.

Secondly, it seemed to me to be untrue. I had intellectual objections to the Christian faith and, rather pretentiously, I called myself a logical determinist. When I was fourteen I wrote an essay in an RE lesson in which I tried to destroy the whole of Christianity and disprove the existence of God. Rather surprisingly, it was put forward for a prize! I had knock-down arguments against the Christian faith and rather enjoyed arguing with Christians, thinking I had won some great victory.

Thirdly, I thought that it was irrelevant. I could not see how something that happened 2,000 years ago and 2,000 miles away in the Middle East could have any relevance to my life in twentieth-century Britain. We often used to sing that much-loved hymn 'Jerusalem' which asks, 'And did those feet in ancient time walk upon England's mountains green?' We all knew that the answer was, 'No, they did not.' It seemed to be totally irrelevant to my life.

I realise, with hindsight, it was partly my fault as I never really listened and was totally ignorant about the Christian faith. There are many people today, in our secularised society, who don't know much about Jesus Christ, or what he did, or anything to do with Christianity. One hospital chaplain listed some of the replies he was given to the question, 'Would you like Holy Communion?' These are some of the answers:

'No thanks, I'm Church of England.'

'No thanks, I asked for Cornflakes.'

'No thanks, I've never been circumcised.'[1]

Christianity is far from boring, it is not untrue and it is not irrelevant. On the contrary, it is exciting, true and relevant. Jesus said, 'I am the way and the truth and the life' (John 14:6). If he was right, and I believe he was, then there can be nothing more important in this life than our response to him.

DIRECTION FOR A LOST WORLD

Men and women were created to live in a relationship with God. Without that relationship there will always be a hunger, an emptiness, a feeling that something is missing. Prince Charles once spoke of his belief that, for all the advances of science, 'there remains deep in the soul (if I dare use that word), a persistent and unconscious anxiety that something is missing, some ingredient that makes life worth living'.

Bernard Levin, perhaps the greatest columnist of this generation, once wrote an article called 'Life's Great Riddle, and No Time to Find Its Meaning'. In it he spoke of the fact that in spite of his great success as a columnist for over twenty years he feared that he might have 'wasted reality in the chase of a dream'. He wrote:

> To put it bluntly, have I time to discover why I was born before I die?. . . I have not managed to answer the question yet, and however many years I have before me they are certainly not as many as there are behind. There is an obvious danger in leaving it too late . . . why do I *have* to know why I was born? Because, of course, I am unable to believe that it was an accident; and if it wasn't one, it must have a meaning.[2]

He is not a Christian and on one occasion wrote, 'For the fourteen thousandth time, I am not a Christian.' Yet he seems to be only too aware of the inadequate answers to the meaning of life. He wrote some years earlier:

> Countries like ours are full of people who have all the material comforts they desire, together with such non-material blessings as a happy family, and yet lead lives of quiet, and at times noisy, desperation,

understanding nothing but the fact that there is a hole inside them and that however much food and drink they pour into it, however many motor cars and television sets they stuff it with, however many well balanced children and loyal friends they parade around the edges of it . . . it aches.[3]

Some people spend much of their lives seeking something that will give meaning and purpose to life. Leo Tolstoy, author of *War and Peace* and *Anna Karenina*, wrote a book called *A Confession* in 1879, in which he tells the story of his search for meaning and purpose in life. He had rejected Christianity as a child. When he left university he sought to get as much pleasure out of life as he could. He entered the social world of Moscow and Petersburg, drinking heavily, living promiscuously, gambling and leading a wild life. But it did not satisfy him.

Then he became ambitious for money. He had inherited an estate and made a large amount of money out of his books. Yet that did not satisfy him either. He sought success, fame and importance. These he also achieved. He wrote what the *Encyclopaedia Britannica* describes as 'one of the two or three greatest novels in world literature'. But he was left asking the question 'Well fine . . . so what?', to which he had no answer.

Then he became ambitious for his family – to give them the best possible life. He married in 1862 and had a kind, loving wife and thirteen children (which, he said, distracted him from any search for the overall meaning of life!). He had achieved all his ambitions and was surrounded by what appeared to be complete happiness. And yet one question brought him to the verge of suicide: 'Is there any meaning in my life which will not be annihilated by the inevitability of death which awaits me?'

He searched for the answer in every field of science and philosophy. The only answer he could find to the question 'Why do I live?' was that 'in the infinity of space and the infinity of time infinitely small particles mutate with infinite complexity'.

As he looked round at his contemporaries he saw that people were not facing up to the first order questions of life ('Where did I come from?', 'Where am I heading?', 'Who am I?', 'What is life about?'). Eventually he found that the peasant people of Russia had been able to answer these questions through their Christian faith and he came to realise that only in Jesus Christ do we find the answer.

Over one hundred years later nothing has changed. Freddie Mercury, the lead singer of the rock group Queen, who died at the end of 1991 wrote in one of his last songs on *The Miracle* album, 'Does anybody know what we are living for?' In spite of the fact that he had amassed a huge fortune and had attracted thousands of fans, he admitted in an interview shortly before his death that he was desperately lonely. He said, 'You can have everything in the world and still be the loneliest man, and that is the most bitter type of loneliness. Success has brought me world idolisation and millions of pounds, but it's prevented me from having the one thing we all need – a loving, ongoing relationship.'

He was right to speak of an 'ongoing relationship' as the one thing we all need. Yet no human relationship will satisfy entirely. Nor can it be completely ongoing. There will always be something missing. That is because we were created to live in a relationship with God. Jesus said, 'I am the way.' He is the only One who can bring us into that relationship with God that goes on into eternity.

When I was a child our family had an old black and white television set. We could never get a very good picture; it was always fuzzy and used to go into lines. We were quite happy with it since we did not know anything different. One day, we discovered that it needed an outside aerial! Suddenly we found that we could get clear and distinct pictures. Our enjoyment was transformed. Life without a relationship with God through Jesus Christ is like the television without the aerial. Some people seem quite happy, because they don't realise that there is something better. Once we have experienced a relationship with God the purpose and meaning of life should become clear. We see things that we have never seen, and it would be foolish to want to return to the old life. We understand why we were made.

REALITY IN A CONFUSED WORLD

Sometimes people say, 'It does not matter what you believe so long as you are sincere.' But it is possible to be sincerely wrong. Adolf Hitler was sincerely wrong. His beliefs destroyed the lives of millions of people. The Yorkshire Ripper believed that he was doing God's will when he killed prostitutes. He too was sincerely wrong. His beliefs affected his behaviour. These are extreme examples, but they make the point that it matters a great deal what we believe, because what we believe will dictate how we live.

Other people's response to a Christian may be, 'It's great for you, but it is not for me.' This is not a logical position. If Christianity is true, it is of vital importance to every one of us. If it is not true, Christians are deluded and it is not 'great for us' – it is very sad and the sooner we are put right the better. As the writer and scholar C. S. Lewis put it, 'Christianity is a statement which, if false, is of *no* importance, and, if true, of infinite importance. The one thing it cannot be is moderately important.'[4]

Is it true? Is there any evidence? Jesus said, 'I am . . . the truth.' Is there any evidence to support his claim? These are some of the questions we will be looking at later in the book. The linchpin of Christianity is the resurrection of Jesus Christ and for that there is ample evidence. Professor Thomas Arnold, who as the headmaster of Rugby School revolutionised the concept of English education, was appointed to the chair of modern history at Oxford University. He was certainly a man well acquainted with the value of evidence in determining historical facts, and he said:

> I have been used for many years to studying the histories of other times, and to examining and weighing the evidence of those who have written about them, and I know of no one fact in the history of mankind which is proved by better and fuller evidence of every sort, to the understanding of a fair inquirer, than the great sign which God has given us that Christ died and rose again from the dead.

As we shall see later in the book, there is a great deal of evidence that Christianity is true. Yet, when Jesus said, 'I am . . . the truth,' he meant more than intellectual truth. The original word for truth carries with it the notion of doing or experiencing the truth. There is something more than an intellectual acceptance of the truth of Christianity, and that is the knowledge of Jesus Christ who is *the* truth.

Suppose that before I met my wife Pippa I had read a book about her. Then, after I had finished reading the book I thought, 'This sounds like a wonderful woman. This is the person I want to marry.' There would be a big difference in my state of mind then –

intellectually convinced that she was a wonderful person – and my state of mind now after the experience of many years of marriage from which I can say, 'I know she is a wonderful person.' When a Christian says, in relation to his faith, 'I know Jesus is the truth,' he does not mean only that he knows intellectually that he is the truth, but that he has experienced Jesus as the truth. As we come into relationship with the One who is the truth, our perceptions change, and we begin to understand the truth about the world around us.

LIFE IN A DARK WORLD

Jesus said, 'I am . . . the life.' In Jesus we find life where previously there has been guilt, addiction, fear and the prospect of death. It is true that all of us were created in the image of God and there is, therefore, something noble about all human beings. However, we are all also fallen – we are born with a propensity to do evil. In every human being the image of God has been to a greater or lesser extent tarnished, and in some cases almost eradicated, by sin. Good and bad, strength and weakness coexist in all human beings. Alexander Solzhenitsyn, the Russian writer, said, 'The line separating good and evil passes, not through states, nor through classes, nor between political parties . . . but right through every human heart and through all human hearts.'

I used to think I was a 'nice' person – because I didn't rob banks or commit other serious crimes. Only when I began to see my life alongside the life of Jesus Christ did I realise how much there was wrong. Many others have had this same experience. C. S. Lewis wrote: 'For the first time I examined myself with a seriously practical purpose. And there I found what appalled me; a zoo of lusts, a bedlam of ambitions, a nursery of fears, a harem of fondled hatreds. My name was Legion.'[5]

We all need forgiveness and only in Christ can it be found. Marghanita Laski, the humanist, debating on television with a Christian, made an amazing confession. She said, 'What I envy most about you Christians is your forgiveness.' Then she added, rather pathetically, 'I have no one to forgive me.'

What Jesus did when he was crucified for us was to pay the penalty for all the things that we have done wrong. We will look at this subject in Chapter 4 in more detail. We will see that he died to remove our guilt, to set us free from addiction, fear and ultimately death. He died instead of us.

If you or I had been the only person in the world, Jesus Christ would have died instead of us to remove our guilt. When our guilt is removed we have a new life.

Jesus not only died for us, he also rose again from the dead for us. In this act he defeated death. Most rational people are aware of the inevitability of death, although today some people make bizarre attempts to avoid it. *The Church of England Newspaper* described one such attempt:

In 1960 Californian millionaire James McGill died. He left detailed instructions that his body should be preserved and frozen in the hope that one day scientists might discover a cure for the disease that killed him. There are hundreds of people in Southern California who have put hopes of one day living again in this process which freezes and preserves human bodies. The latest development in Cryonics technology is called neuro-suspension which preserves just the human head. One reason why it is becoming popular is that it is much cheaper than preserving and maintaining a whole body. It reminds me of Woody Allen in *Sleeper*, where he preserved his nose.[6]

Such attempts to avoid the inevitability of death are plainly absurd and, indeed, unnecessary. Jesus came to bring us 'eternal life'. Eternal life is a quality of life which comes from living in a relationship with God and Jesus Christ (John 17:3). Jesus never promised anyone an easy life, but he promised fullness of life (John 10:10). This new quality of life starts now and goes on into eternity. Our time on earth is relatively short, but eternity is vast. Through Jesus, who said, 'I am . . . the life' we can not only enjoy fullness of life here, but we can be sure that it will never end.

Christianity is not boring; it is about living life to the full. It is not untrue; it is *the* truth. It is not irrelevant; it transforms the whole of our lives. The theologian and philosopher Paul Tillich described the human condition as one that always involves three fears: fear about meaninglessness, fear about death and fear about guilt. Jesus Christ meets each of these fears head on. He is vital to every one of us because he is 'the way, and the truth, and the life'.

2

Who Is Jesus?

A missionary working among children in the Middle East was driving her jeep down a road when she ran out of petrol. She had no jerrycan in her car. All she could find was a potty. She walked a mile down the road to the nearest petrol station and filled the potty with petrol. As she was pouring the petrol into the tank, a very large Cadillac drew up occupied by wealthy oil sheikhs. They were absolutely fascinated at seeing her pouring the contents of the potty into the jeep. One of them opened the window and said, 'Excuse me! My friend and I, although we do not share your religion, greatly admire your faith!'

Some people see becoming a Christian as a blind leap of faith – the type of faith that would be needed to expect a car to run on the usual contents of a potty. There is indeed a step of faith required. However, it is not a blind leap of faith, but a step of faith based on firm historical evidence. In this chapter I want to examine some of that historical evidence.

I am told that in a communist Russian dictionary Jesus is described as 'a mythical figure who never existed'. No serious historian could maintain that position today. There is a great deal of evidence for Jesus' existence. This comes not only from the

Gospels and other Christian writings, but also from non-Christian sources. For example, the Roman historians Tacitus (directly) and Suetonius (indirectly) both write about him. The Jewish historian Josephus, born in AD 37, describes Jesus and his followers thus:

> Now there was about this time, Jesus, a wise man, if it be lawful to call him a man, for he was a doer of wonderful works – a teacher of such men as receive the truth with pleasure. He drew over to him both many of the Jews, and many of the Gentiles. He was [the] Christ; and when Pilate, at the suggestion of the principal men amongst us, had condemned him to the cross, those that loved him at first did not forsake him, for he appeared to them alive again the third day, as the divine prophets had foretold these and ten thousand other wonderful things concerning him; and the tribe of Christians so named after him, are not extinct at this day.[7]

So there is evidence outside the New Testament for the existence of Jesus. Furthermore, the evidence in the New Testament is very strong. Sometimes people say, 'The New Testament was written a long time ago. How do we know that what they wrote down has not been changed over the years?'

The answer is that we do know, very accurately through the science of textual criticism, what the New Testament writers wrote. Essentially the more texts we have, the less doubt there is about the original. The late Professor F. F. Bruce (who was Rylands professor of biblical criticism and exegesis at the University of Manchester) shows in his book *Are the New Testament Documents Reliable?* how wealthy the New Testament is in manuscript attestation by comparing its texts with other historical works.

The table below summarises the facts and shows the extent of the New Testament evidence.

Work	When written	Earliest copy	Time span (yrs)	No. of copies
Herodotus	488-428 BC	AD 900	1,300	8
Thucydides	c. 460-400 BC	c. AD 900	1,300	8
Tacitus	AD 100	1100	1,000	20
Caesar's *Gallic War*	58-50 BC	AD 900	950	9-10
Livy's *Roman History*	59 BC-AD 17	AD 900	900	20
New Testament	AD 40-100	AD 130 (full manuscripts AD 350)	300	5,000+ Greek 10,000 Latin 9,300 others

F. F. Bruce points out that for Caesar's *Gallic War* we have nine or ten copies and the oldest was written some 900 years later than Caesar's day. For Livy's *Roman History* we have not more than twenty copies, the earliest of which comes from around AD 900. Of the fourteen books of the histories of Tacitus only twenty copies survive; of the sixteen books of his *Annals*, ten portions of his two great historical works depend entirely on two manuscripts, one of the ninth century and one of the eleventh century. The history of Thucydides is known almost entirely from eight manuscripts belonging to c. AD 900. The same is true of the history of Herodotus. Yet no classical scholar doubts the authenticity of these works, in spite of the large time gap and the relatively small number of manuscripts.

As regards the New Testament we have a great wealth of material. The New Testament was probably written between AD 40 and AD 100. We have excellent full manuscripts of the whole New Testament dating from as early as AD 350 (a time span of only 300 years), papyri containing most of the New Testament writings dating from the third century and even a fragment of John's Gospel dating from about AD 130. There are over 5,000 Greek manuscripts, over 10,000 Latin manuscripts and 9,300 other manuscripts, as well as over 36,000 citings in the writings of the early church fathers. As one of the greatest ever textual critics, F. J. A. Hort, said, 'In the variety and fullness of the evidence on which it rests, the text of the New Testament stands absolutely and unapproachably alone among ancient prose writings.'[8]

F. F. Bruce summarises the evidence by quoting Sir Frederic Kenyon, a leading scholar in this area:

> The interval then between the dates of original composition and the earliest extant evidence becomes so small as to be in fact negligible, and the last foundation for any doubt that the Scriptures have come down to us substantially as they were written has now been removed. Both the *authenticity* and the *general integrity* of the books of the New Testament may be regarded as finally established.[9]

We know from evidence outside and inside the New Testament that Jesus existed.[10] But who is he? I heard Martin Scorsese say on television that he made the film *The Last Temptation of Christ* in order to show that Jesus was a real human being. Yet that is not the issue at the moment. Few people today would doubt that Jesus was fully human. He had a human body; he was sometimes tired (John 4:6) and hungry (Matthew 4:2). He had human emotions; he was angry (Mark 11:15-17), he loved (Mark 10:21) and he was sad (John 11:35). He had human experiences; he was tempted (Mark 1:13), he learned (Luke 2:52), he worked (Mark 6:3) and he obeyed his parents (Luke 2:51).

What many say today is that Jesus was *only* a human being – albeit a great religious teacher. The comedian Billy Connolly spoke for many when he said, 'I can't believe in Christianity, but I think Jesus was a wonderful man.'

What evidence is there to suggest that Jesus was more than just a wonderful man or a great moral teacher? The answer, as we shall see, is that there is a great deal of evidence. This evidence supports the Christian contention that Jesus was and is the unique Son of God. Indeed, he is God the Son, the second Person of the Trinity.

WHAT DID HE SAY ABOUT HIMSELF?

Some people say, 'Jesus never claimed to be God.' Indeed, it is true that Jesus did not go round saying the words, 'I am God.' Yet when one looks at all he taught and claimed, there is little doubt that he was conscious of being a person whose identity was God.

Teaching centred on himself
One of the fascinating things about Jesus is that so much of his teaching was centred on himself. He said to people, in effect, 'If you want to have a relationship with God you need to come to me' (see John 14:6). It is through a relationship with him that we encounter God.

There is a hunger deep within the human heart. The leading psychologists of the twentieth century have all recognised this. Freud said, 'People are hungry for love.' Jung said, 'People are hungry for security.' Adler said, 'People are hungry for significance.' Jesus said, 'I am the bread of life' (John 6:35). In other words, 'If you want your hunger satisfied, come to me.'

Many people are walking in darkness, depression, disillusionment and despair. They are looking for direction. Jesus said, 'I am the light of the world. Whoever follows me will never walk in darkness, but will have the light of life' (John 8:12). Someone said to me after they had become a Christian, 'It was as if the light had suddenly been turned on and I could see things for the first time.'

Many are fearful of death. One woman said to me that sometimes she couldn't sleep and that she would wake up in a cold sweat, frightened about death, because she didn't know what was going to happen when she died. Jesus said, 'I am the resurrection and the life. Those who believe in me will live, even though they die; and whoever lives and believes in me will never die' (John 11:25-26).

So many are burdened by worries, anxieties, fears and guilt. Jesus said, 'Come to me, all you who are weary and burdened, and I will give you rest' (Matthew 11:28). They are not sure how to run their lives or who they should follow. I can remember, before I was a Christian, that I would be impressed by someone and want to be like them, and then by a different person and follow them. Jesus said, 'Follow *me*' (Mark 1:17).

He said to receive him was to receive God (Matthew 10:40), to welcome him was to welcome God (Mark 9:37) and to have seen him was to have seen God (John 14:9). A child once drew a picture and her mother asked what she was doing. The child said, 'I am drawing a picture of God.' The mother said, 'Don't be silly. You can't draw a picture of God. No one knows what God looks like.' The child replied, 'Well, they will do by the time I have finished!'

Jesus said in effect, 'If you want to know what God looks like, look at me.'

Indirect claims

Jesus said a number of things which, although not direct claims to be God, show that he regarded himself as being in the same position as God, as we will see in the examples which follow.

Jesus' claim to be able to forgive sins is well known. For example, on one occasion he said to a man who was paralysed, 'Son, your sins are forgiven' (Mark 2:5). The reaction of the religious leaders was, 'Why does this fellow talk like that? He's blaspheming! Who can forgive sins but God alone?' Jesus went on to prove that he did have the authority to forgive sins by healing the paralysed man. This claim to be able to forgive sins is indeed an astonishing claim.

C. S. Lewis puts it well when he says in his book *Mere Christianity*:

> One part of the claim tends to slip past us unnoticed because we have heard it so often that we no longer see what it amounts to. I mean the claim to forgive sins: any sins. Now unless the speaker is God, this is really so preposterous as to be comic. We can all understand how a man forgives offences against himself. You tread on my toes and I forgive you, you steal my money and I forgive you. But what should we make of a man, himself unrobbed and untrodden on, who announced that he forgave you for treading on other men's toes and stealing other men's money? Asinine fatuity is the kindest description we should give of his conduct. Yet this is what Jesus did. He told people that their sins were forgiven, and never waited to consult all the other people whom their sins had undoubtedly injured. He unhesitatingly behaved as if He was the party chiefly concerned, the person chiefly offended in all offences. This makes sense only if He really was the God whose laws are broken and whose love is wounded in every sin. In the mouth of any speaker who is not God, these words would imply what I can only

regard as a silliness and conceit unrivalled by any other character in history.[11]

Another extraordinary claim that Jesus made was that one day he would judge the world (Matthew 25:31-32). He said he would return and 'sit on his throne in heavenly glory' (v. 31). All the nations would be gathered before him. He would pass judgement on them. Some would receive an inheritance prepared for them since the creation of the world and eternal life, but others would suffer the punishment of being separated from him for ever.

Jesus said he would decide what happens to every one of us at the end of time. Not only would he be the Judge, he would also be the criterion of judgement. What happens to us on the Day of Judgement depends on how we respond to Jesus in this life (Matthew 25:40, 45). Suppose the vicar of your local church were to get up in the pulpit and say, 'On the Day of Judgement you will all appear before me and I will decide your eternal destiny. What happens to you will depend on how you've treated me and my followers.' For a mere human being to make such a claim would be preposterous. Here we have another indirect claim to have the identity of Almighty God.

Direct claims
When the question was put to him, 'Are you the Christ, the Son of the Blessed One?' Jesus said, 'I am . . . and you will see the Son of Man sitting at the right hand of the Mighty One and coming on the clouds of heaven.' The high priest tore his clothes. 'Why do we need any more witnesses?' he asked. 'You have heard the blasphemy. What do you think?' (Mark 14:61-64). In this account it appears Jesus was condemned to death for the assertion he made about himself. A claim tantamount to a claim to be God was blasphemy in Jewish eyes, worthy of death.

On one occasion, when the Jews started to stone Jesus, he asked, 'Why are you stoning me?' They replied that they were stoning him for blasphemy 'because you, a mere man, *claim to be God*' (John 10:33, italics mine). His enemies clearly thought that this was exactly what he was declaring.

When Thomas, one of his disciples, knelt down before Jesus and said, 'My Lord and my God' (John 20:28), Jesus didn't turn to him and say, 'No, no, don't say that; I am not God.' He said, 'Because you have seen me, you have believed; blessed are those who have not seen and yet have believed' (John 20:29). He rebuked Thomas for being so slow to get the point.

If somebody makes claims like these they need to be tested. There are all sorts of people who make all kinds of claims. The mere fact that somebody claims to be someone does not mean that they are right. There are many people, some in psychiatric hospitals, who are deluded. They think they are Napoleon or the Pope, but they are not.

So how can we test people's claims? Jesus claimed to be the unique Son of God – God made flesh. There are three logical possibilities. If the claims were untrue, either he knew they were untrue – in which case he was an imposter, and an evil one at that. That is the first possibility. Or he did not know – in which case he was deluded; indeed, he was insane. That is the second possibility. The third possibility is that the claims were true.

C. S. Lewis pointed out that: 'A man who was merely a man and said the sort of things Jesus said would not be a great moral teacher.' He would either be insane or else he would be 'the Devil of Hell'. 'You must make your choice,' he writes. Either Jesus was, and is, the Son of God or else he was insane or evil but, C. S. Lewis goes on, 'let us not come up with any patronising nonsense about His being a great human teacher. He has not left that open to us. He did not intend to.'[12]

WHAT EVIDENCE IS THERE TO SUPPORT WHAT HE SAID?

In order to assess which of these three possibilities is right we need to examine the evidence we have about his life.

His teaching

The teaching of Jesus is widely acknowledged to be the greatest teaching that has ever fallen from human lips. Some who are not Christians say, 'I love the Sermon on the Mount; I live by it.' (If they were to read it they would realise that this is easier to say than to do, but they acknowledge that the Sermon on the Mount is great teaching.)

Bernard Ramm, an American professor of theology, said this about the teachings of Jesus:

> They are read more, quoted more, loved more, believed more, and translated more because they are the greatest words ever spoken . . . Their greatness lies in the pure lucid spirituality in dealing clearly, definitively, and authoritatively with the greatest problems that throb in the human breast . . . No other man's words have the appeal of Jesus' words because no other man can answer these fundamental human questions as Jesus answered them. They are the kind of words and the kind of answers we would expect God to give.[13]

His teaching is the foundation of our entire civilisation in the West. Many of the laws in this country were originally based on the teachings of Jesus. We are making progress in virtually every field of science and technology. We travel faster and know more, and yet in nearly 2,000 years no one has improved on the moral teaching of Jesus Christ. Could that teaching really have come from someone evil or insane?

His works

Jesus said that the miracles he performed were in themselves evidence that 'the Father is in me, and I in the Father' (John 10:38).

Jesus must have been the most extraordinary person to have around. Sometimes people say that Christianity is boring. Well, it was not boring being with Jesus.

When he went to a party, he turned water into wine (John 2:1-11). He received one man's picnic and multiplied it so that it could feed thousands (Mark 6:30-44). He had control over the elements and could speak to the wind and the waves and thereby stop a storm (Mark 4:35-41). He carried out the most remarkable healings: opening blind eyes, causing the deaf and dumb to hear and speak and enabling the paralysed to walk again. When he visited a hospital a man who had been an invalid for thirty-eight years was able to pick up his bed and walk (John 5:1-9). He set people free from evil forces which had dominated their lives. On occasions, he even brought those who had died back to life (John 11:38-44).

Yet it was not just his miracles that made his work so impressive. It was his love, especially for the loveless (such as the lepers and the prostitutes), which seemed to motivate all that he did. The supreme demonstration of his love for us was shown on the cross (which, as we shall see in the next chapter, was the chief reason for his coming to earth). When they tortured him and nailed him to the cross he said, 'Father, forgive them, for they do not know what they are doing' (Luke 22:34). Surely these are not the activities of an evil or deluded man?

His character

The character of Jesus has impressed millions who would not call themselves Christians. For example, Bernard Levin wrote of Jesus:

Is not the nature of Christ, in the words of the New Testament, enough to pierce to the soul anyone with a soul to be pierced? . . . he still looms over the world, his message still clear, his pity still infinite, his consolation still effective, his words still full of glory, wisdom and love.[14]

One of my favourite descriptions of the character of Jesus comes from the former Lord Chancellor, Lord Hailsham. In his autobiographical *The Door Wherein I Went* he describes how the person of Jesus came alive to him when he was at university:

The first thing we must learn about him is that we should have been absolutely entranced by his company. Jesus was irresistibly attractive as a man . . . What they crucified was a young man, vital, full of life and the joy of it, the Lord of life itself, and even more the Lord of laughter, someone so utterly attractive that people followed him for the sheer fun of it . . . the Twentieth Century needs to recapture the vision of this glorious and happy man whose mere presence filled his companions with delight. No pale Galilean he, but a veritable Pied Piper of Hamelin who would have the children laughing all round him and squealing with pleasure and joy as he picked them up.[15]

Here was someone who exemplified supreme unselfishness but never self-pity; humility but not weakness; joy but never at another's expense; kindness but not indulgence. He was a person in whom even his enemies could find no fault and where friends who knew him well said he was without sin. Surely no one could suggest that a man with a character like that was evil or unbalanced?

His fulfilment of Old Testament prophecy
Wilbur Smith, the American writer on theological topics, said:

The ancient world had many different devices for determining the future, known as divination, but not in the entire gamut of Greek and

Latin literature, even though they used the words prophet and prophecy, can we find any real specific prophecy of a great historic event to come in the distant future, nor any prophecy of a Saviour to arrive in the human race . . . Mohammedanism cannot point to any prophecies of the coming of Mohammed uttered hundreds of years before his birth. Neither can the founders of any cult in this country rightly identify any ancient text specifically foretelling their appearance.[16]

Yet in the case of Jesus, he fulfilled over 300 prophecies (spoken by different voices over 500 years), including twenty-nine major prophecies fulfilled in a single day – the day he died. Although some of these prophecies may have found fulfilment at one level in the prophet's own day, they found their ultimate fulfilment in Jesus Christ.

I suppose it could be suggested that Jesus was a clever con man who deliberately set out to fulfil these prophecies in order to show that he was the Messiah foretold in the Old Testament.

The problem with that suggestion is, first, the sheer number of them would have made it extremely difficult. Secondly, humanly speaking he had no control over many of the events. For example, the exact manner of his death was foretold in the Old Testament (Isaiah 53), the place of his burial and even the place of his birth (Micah 5:2). Suppose Jesus had been a con man wanting to fulfil all these prophecies. It would have been a bit late by the time he discovered the place in which he was supposed to have been born!

His resurrection
The physical resurrection from the dead of Jesus Christ is the cornerstone of Christianity. But what is the evidence that it really happened? I want to summarise the evidence under four main headings.

1. His absence from the tomb. Many theories have been put forward to explain the fact that Jesus' body was absent from the tomb on the first Easter Day, but none of them is very convincing.

First, it has been suggested that Jesus did not die on the cross. There was once a headline in a major UK newspaper: 'Jesus did not die on the cross'. Dr Trevor Lloyd Davies claimed that Jesus was still alive when he was taken from the cross and that he later recovered.

Jesus had undergone a Roman flogging, under which many died. He had been nailed to a cross for six hours. Could a man in this condition push away a stone weighing probably a ton and a half? The soldiers were clearly convinced that he was dead or they would not have taken his body down. If they had allowed a prisoner to escape, they would have been liable to the death penalty.

Furthermore, when the soldiers discovered that Jesus was already dead, 'one of the soldiers pierced Jesus' side with a spear, bringing a sudden flow of blood and water' (John 19:34). This appears to be the separation of clot and serum which we know today is strong medical evidence that Jesus was dead. John did not write it for that reason; he would not have possessed that knowledge, which makes it even more powerful evidence that Jesus was indeed dead.

Secondly, it has been argued that the disciples stole the body. Some have suggested that the disciples stole the body and began a rumour that Jesus had risen from the dead. Leaving aside the fact that the tomb was guarded, this theory is psychologically improbable. The disciples were depressed and disillusioned at the time of Jesus' death. It would have needed something extraordinary to transform the apostle Peter into the man who preached at Pentecost when 3,000 people were converted.

In addition, when one considers how much they had to suffer for what they believed (floggings, torture, and for some even death), it seems inconceivable that they would be prepared to endure all that for something they knew to be untrue. I have a friend who was a scientist at Cambridge University who became a Christian because, as he examined the evidence, he was convinced that the disciples would not have been willing to die for what they knew to be a lie.

Thirdly, some have said that the authorities stole the body. This seems the least probable theory of all. If the authorities had stolen the body, why did they not produce it when they were trying to quash the rumour that Jesus had risen from the dead?

Perhaps the most fascinating piece of evidence relating to Jesus' absence from the tomb is John's description of the grave-clothes. In a way, the 'empty tomb' is a misnomer. When Peter and John went to the tomb they saw the grave-clothes which were, as the Christian apologist Josh McDowell put it in *The Resurrection Factor*, 'like the empty chrysalis of a caterpillar's cocoon' – when the butterfly has emerged.[17] It was as if Jesus had simply passed through the grave-clothes. Not surprisingly, John 'saw and believed' (John 20:8).

2. His appearances to the disciples. Were these hallucinations? The Concise Oxford Dictionary describes a hallucination as an 'apparent perception of an external object not actually present'. Hallucinations normally occur in highly strung, highly imaginative and very nervous people, or in people who are sick or on drugs. The disciples do not fit into any of these categories. Burly fishermen, tax collectors and sceptics like Thomas are unlikely to hallucinate. People who hallucinate would be unlikely suddenly to stop doing so. Jesus appeared to his disciples on eleven different occasions over a period of six weeks. The number of occasions and the sudden cessation make the hallucination theory highly improbable.

Furthermore, over 500 people saw the risen Jesus. It is possible for one person to hallucinate. Maybe it is possible for two or three people to share the same hallucination. But is it likely that 500 people would all share the same hallucination?

Finally, hallucinations are subjective. There is no objective reality – it is like seeing a ghost. Jesus could be touched, he ate a piece of broiled fish (Luke 24:42-43) and on one occasion he cooked breakfast for the disciples (John 21:1-14). Peter says, '[They] ate and drank with him after he rose from the dead' (Acts 10:41). He held long conversations with them, teaching them many things about the kingdom of God (Acts 1:3).

3. The immediate effect. The fact of Jesus rising from the dead, as one would expect, had a dramatic impact on the world. The church was born and grew at a tremendous rate. As Michael Green, writer of many popular and scholarly works, puts it:

> [The] church . . . beginning from a handful of uneducated fishermen and tax gatherers, swept across the whole known world in the next three hundred years. It is a perfectly amazing story of peaceful revolution that has no parallel in the history of the world. It came about because Christians were able to say to inquirers: 'Jesus did not only die for you. He is alive! You can meet him and discover for yourself the reality we are talking about!' They did, and joined the church and the church, born from that Easter grave, spread everywhere.[18]

4. Christian experience. Countless millions of people down the ages have experienced the risen Jesus Christ. They consist of people of every colour, race, tribe, continent and nationality. They come from different economic, social and intellectual backgrounds. Yet they all unite in a common experience of the risen Jesus Christ. Wilson Carlile, who was head of the Church Army in this country, was preaching at Hyde Park Corner. He was saying, 'Jesus Christ is alive today.' One of the hecklers shouted out to him, 'How do you know?' Wilson Carlile replied, 'Because I was speaking to him for half an hour this morning!'

Millions of Christians all over the world today are experiencing a relationship with the risen Jesus Christ. Over the last eighteen years I too have found in my experience that Jesus Christ is alive today. I have experienced his love, his power and the reality of a relationship which convinces me that he really is alive.

The evidence that Jesus rose from the dead is very extensive. A former Chief Justice of England, Lord Darling, said, 'In its favour as living truth there exists such overwhelming evidence, positive and negative, factual and circumstantial, that no intelligent jury in the world could fail to bring in a verdict that the resurrection story is true.'[19]

We saw when we looked earlier in the chapter at what Jesus said about himself that there were only three realistic possibilities – either he was and is the Son of God, or else deluded or something more sinister. When one looks at the evidence it does not make sense to say that he was insane or evil. The whole weight of his teaching, his works, his character, his fulfilment of Old Testament prophecy and his conquest of death make those suggestions absurd, illogical and unbelievable. On the other hand, they lend the strongest possible support to Jesus' own consciousness of being a man whose identity was God.

In conclusion, as C. S. Lewis pointed out: 'We are faced then with a frightening alternative.' Either Jesus was (and is) exactly what he said, or else he was insane or something worse. To C. S. Lewis it seemed clear that he could have been neither insane nor evil and thus he concludes, 'However strange or terrifying or unlikely it may seem, I have to accept the view that he was and is God.'[20]

3

Why Did Jesus Die?

Many people today go around with a cross on their earrings, bracelet or necklace. We are so used to seeing this that we are not shocked by it. We might be if we saw someone wearing a gallows or an electric chair on a chain; but the cross was just as much a form of execution. Indeed, it was one of the cruellest forms of execution known to humankind. It was abolished in AD 315 because even the Romans considered it too inhumane.

Yet the cross has always been regarded as the symbol of the Christian faith. A high proportion of the Gospels is about the death of Jesus. Much of the rest of the New Testament is concerned with explaining what happened on the cross. The central service of the church, the Communion service, centres on the broken body and shed blood of Jesus. Churches are often built in the shape of a cross. When the apostle Paul went to Corinth he said, 'I resolved to know nothing while I was with you except Jesus Christ and him crucified' (1 Corinthians 2:2). Most leaders who have influenced nations or even changed the world, are remembered for the impact of their lives. Jesus, who more than any other person changed the face of world history, is remembered not so much for his life but for his death.

Why is there such concentration on the death of Jesus? What is the difference between his death and the death of Socrates, or one of the martyrs, or war heroes? What did it achieve? What does it mean when the New Testament says he died 'for our sins'? Why did he die? The answer in a nutshell is 'because God loves you'. 'The whole Bible,' St Augustine observed, 'does nothing but tell of God's love.'[21] Raniero Cantalamessa, preacher to the Pope, said, 'The love of God is the answer to all the "whys" in the Bible.' It is because 'God so loved the world' that he sent his one and only Son to die for us so that 'whoever believes in him shall not perish but have eternal life' (John 3:16).

THE PROBLEM

Sometimes people say, 'I have no need for Christianity.' They say something along the lines of, 'I am quite happy, my life is full and I try to be nice to other people and lead a good life.' In order to understand why Jesus died we have to go back and look at the greatest problem which confronts every person.

If we are honest, we would all have to admit that we do things which we know are wrong. Paul wrote: 'All have sinned and fall short of the glory of God' (Romans 3:23). In other words, relative to God's standards we all fall a long way short. If we compare ourselves to armed robbers or child molesters or even our neighbours, we may think we come off quite well. But when we compare ourselves to Jesus Christ, we see how far short we fall. Somerset Maugham once said, 'If I wrote down every thought I have ever thought and every deed I have ever done, men would call me a monster of depravity.'

The essence of sin is a rebellion against God – our ignoring God in the sense of behaving as if he doesn't exist (Genesis 3) with the result that we are cut off from him. Like the Prodigal Son (Luke 15), we find ourselves far from our Father's home and with our lives in a mess. Sometimes people say, 'If we are all in the same boat, does it really matter?' The answer is that it does matter because of the consequences of sin in our lives, which can be summarised under four headings.

The pollution of sin

Jesus said, 'What comes out of you is what makes you "unclean". For from within, out of your hearts, come evil thoughts, sexual immorality, theft, murder, adultery, greed, malice, deceit, lewdness, envy, slander, arrogance and folly. All these evils come from inside and make you "unclean"' (Mark 7:20-23). These things pollute our lives.

You may say, 'I do not do most of these things.' But one of them alone is enough to mess up our lives. We might wish the Ten Commandments were like an examination paper in which we only have to 'attempt any three' of them. The New Testament says that if we break *any* part of the Law we are guilty of breaking all of it (James 2:10). It is not possible, for example, to have a 'reasonably clean' driving licence. Either it is clean or it is not. One driving offence stops it from being a clean licence. So it is with us. One offence makes our lives unclean.

The power of sin

The things we do wrong have an addictive power. Jesus said, 'Everyone who sins is a slave to sin' (John 8:34). It is easier to see this in some areas of our wrong-doing than with others. For example, it is well-known that if someone takes a hard drug like heroin, it soon becomes an addiction.

It is also possible to be addicted to bad temper, envy, arrogance, pride, selfishness, slander or sexual immorality. We can become addicted to patterns of thought or behaviour which, on our own, we cannot break. This is the slavery which Jesus spoke about and which has a destructive power in our lives.

Bishop J. C. Ryle, a former bishop of Liverpool, once wrote:

Each and all [sins] have crowds of unhappy prisoners bound hand and foot in their chains . . . The wretched prisoners . . . boast sometimes that they are eminently free . . . There is no slavery like this. Sin is indeed the hardest of all task-masters. Misery and disappointment by the way, despair and hell in the end – these are the only wages that sin pays to its servants.[22]

The penalty for sin

There is something in human nature which cries out for justice. When we see children molested, old people attacked in their homes or babies battered, we long for the people who have done these things to be caught and punished. Often our motives may be mixed: there may be an element of revenge. But there is such a thing as justifiable anger. We are right to feel that sins should be punished; that people who do such things should not get away with it.

It is not just other people's sins that deserve punishment; it is our own as well. One day we will all be subject to the judgement of God. St Paul tells us that 'the wages of sin is death' (Romans 6:23).

The partition of sin

The death Paul speaks of is not only physical. It is a spiritual death which results in eternal isolation from God. This cutting off from God begins now. The prophet Isaiah proclaimed, 'Surely the arm of the Lord is not too short to save, nor his ear too dull to hear. But your iniquities have separated you from your God; your sins have hidden his face from you, so that he will not hear' (Isaiah 59:1-2). The things we do wrong cause this barrier.

THE SOLUTION

We all have a need to deal with the problem of sin in our lives. The greater our understanding of our need the more we will appreciate what God has done. The Lord Chancellor, Lord Mackay of Clashfern, wrote: 'The central theme of our faith is the sacrifice of himself by our Lord Jesus Christ on the cross for our sins. . . . The deeper our appreciation of our own need the greater will be our love for the Lord Jesus and, therefore, the more fervent our desire to serve him.'[23] The good news of Christianity is that God loves us and he did not leave us in the mess that we make of our own lives. He came to earth, in the person of his Son Jesus, to die instead of us (2 Corinthians 5:21; Galatians 3:13). This has been called the 'self-substitution of God'.[24] In the words of the apostle Peter, '*He* himself bore *our* sins in *his* body on the tree . . . by *his* wounds you have been healed' (1 Peter 2:24, italics mine).

On 31 July 1991 a remarkable event was celebrated. On the last day of July 1941 the Auschwitz sirens announced the escape of a prisoner. As a reprisal, ten of his fellow prisoners would die – a long, slow starvation, buried alive in a specially constructed, concrete bunker.

So all day, tortured by sun, hunger and fear, the men waited as the German commandant and his Gestapo assistant walked between the ranks to select, quite arbitrarily, the chosen ten. As the commandant pointed to one man, Francis Gajowniczek, he cried out in despair, 'My poor wife and children.' At that moment the unimpressive figure of a man with sunken eyes and round glasses in wire frames stepped out of line and took off his cap. 'What does this Polish pig want?' asked the commandant.

'I am a Catholic priest; I want to die for that man. I am old, he has a wife and children . . . I have no one,' said Father Maximilian Kolbe.

'Accepted,' retorted the commandant, and moved on.

That night, nine men and one priest went to the starvation bunker. Normally they would tear each other apart like cannibals. Not so this time. While they had strength, lying naked on the floor, the men prayed and sang hymns. After two weeks, three of the men and Father Maximilian were still alive. The bunker was required for others, so on 14 August, the remaining four were disposed of. At 12.50 pm, after two weeks in the starvation bunker and still conscious, the Polish priest was finally given an injection of phenol and died at the age of forty-seven.

On 10 October 1982 in St Peter's Square, Rome, Father Maximilian's death was put in its proper perspective. Present in the crowd of 150,000 was Francis Gajowniczek, his wife, his children, and his children's children – for indeed, many had been saved by that one man. The Pope describing Father Maximilian's death said, 'This was victory won over all the systems of contempt and hate in man – a victory like that won by our Lord Jesus Christ.'[25]

Jesus' death was, indeed, even more amazing because Jesus died, not just for one man, but for every single individual in the world.

Jesus came as our substitute. He endured crucifixion for us. Cicero described crucifixion as 'the most cruel and hideous of tortures'. Jesus was stripped and tied to a whipping post. He was flogged with four or five thongs of leather interwoven with sharp jagged bone and lead. Eusebius, the third-century church historian, described Roman flogging in these terms: the sufferer's 'veins were laid bare, and . . . the very muscles, sinews and bowels of the victim were open to exposure'. He was then taken to the Praetorium where a crown of thorns was thrust onto his head. He was mocked by a battalion of about 600 men and hit about the face and head. He was then forced to carry a heavy cross bar on his bleeding shoulders until he collapsed, and Simon of Cyrene was press-ganged into carrying it for him.

When they reached the site of crucifixion, he was again stripped naked. He was laid on the cross, and six-inch nails were driven into his forearms, just above the wrist. His knees were twisted sideways so that the ankles could be nailed between the tibia and the Achilles' tendon. He was lifted up on the cross which was then dropped into a socket in the ground. There he was left to hang in intense heat and unbearable thirst, exposed to the ridicule of the crowd. He hung there in unthinkable pain for six hours while his life slowly drained away.

Yet the worst part of his suffering was not the physical trauma of torture and crucifixion nor even the emotional pain of being rejected by the world and deserted by his friends, but the spiritual agony of being cut off from his Father for us – as he carried our sins.

Jesus' victory was total – he died not just for one person but for all of us – and it was also costly. In all four Gospels, we hear of Jesus' agony in the Garden of Gethsemane, alone, crying out to his Father, 'Abba, Father . . . take this cup from me. Yet not what I will, but what you will' (Mark 14:36).

Raniero Cantalamessa writes:

In the Bible the image of the cup almost always evokes the idea of God's wrath against sin. . . Wherever sin exists, God's judgment cannot but be focussed on it, otherwise God would reach a compromise with sin and the very distinction itself between good and evil would no longer exist. Now, Jesus in Gethsemane is. . . man 'made sin'. Christ, it is written, died 'for sinners'; he died in their place and not only in their favour. . . he is, therefore, 'responsible' for all, the guilty one before God! It is against him that God's wrath is 'revealed' and that is what 'drinking the cup' means.[26]

THE RESULT

Like a beautiful diamond the cross has many facets. On the cross, the powers of evil were disarmed (Colossians 2:15). Death and demonic powers were defeated. On the cross, God revealed his love for us. He showed that he is not a God who is aloof from suffering. He is 'the crucified God' (as the title of the book by the German theologian Jürgen Moltmann puts it). He has entered our world and knows and understands all about suffering. On the cross Jesus sets us an example of self-sacrificial love (1 Peter 2:21). Each of these aspects deserves a chapter of its own, which space does not allow. I want to concentrate here on four images that the New Testament uses to describe what Jesus did on the cross for us.[27] As John Stott, well-known author and Rector Emeritus of All Souls Langham Place, points out, each of them is taken from a different area of day-to-day life.

The first image comes from the *temple.* In the Old Testament, very careful laws were laid down as to how sins should be dealt with. There was a whole system of sacrifices which demonstrated the seriousness of sin and the need for cleansing from it.

In a typical case the sinner would take an animal. The animal was to be as near perfection as possible. The sinner would lay his hands on the animal and confess his sins. Thus the sins were seen to pass from the sinner to the animal which was then killed.

The writer of Hebrews points out that it is 'impossible for the blood of bulls and goats to take away sins' (Hebrews 10:4). It was only a picture or a 'shadow' (Hebrews 10:1). The reality came with the sacrifice of Jesus. Only the blood of Christ, our substitute, can take away our sin, because he alone was the perfect sacrifice since he alone lived a perfect life. His blood purifies us from all sin (1 John 1:7) and removes *the pollution of sin.*

The second image comes from *the market-place.* Debt is not a problem confined to the present day; it was a problem in the ancient world as well. If someone had serious debts, he might be forced to sell himself into slavery in order to pay them off. Suppose a man was standing in the market-place, offering himself as a slave. Someone might have pity on him and ask, 'How much do you owe?' The debtor might say, '10,000.' Suppose the customer offers to pay the 10,000 and then lets him go free. In doing so, he would be 'redeeming him' by paying a 'ransom price'.

In a similar way for us 'redemption . . . came by Jesus Christ' (Romans 3:24). Jesus by his death on the cross paid the ransom price (Mark 10:45). In this way, we are set free from the power of sin. This is true freedom. Jesus said, 'If the Son sets you free, you will be free indeed' (John 8:36). It is not that we never sin again, but that sin's hold over us is broken.

Billy Nolan was an alcoholic for thirty-five years. For twenty years he sat outside Holy Trinity Brompton drinking alcohol, begging for money. On 13 May 1990, he looked in the mirror and said, 'You're not the Billy Nolan I once knew.' To use his own expression, he asked the Lord Jesus Christ into his life and made a covenant with him that he would never drink alcohol again. He has not touched a drop since. His life is transformed. He radiates the love and joy of Christ. I once said to him, 'Billy, you look happy.' He replied, 'I am happy because I am free. Life is like a maze and at last I have found a way out through Jesus Christ.' Jesus' death on the cross made this freedom from *the power of sin* possible.

The third image comes from *the law court*. Paul says that through Christ's death 'we have been justified' (Romans 5:1). Justification is a legal term. If you went to court and were acquitted, you were justified. There is one illustration that particularly helped me to understand what this means.

Two people went through school and university together and developed a close friendship. Life went on and they went their different ways and lost contact. One went on to become a judge, while the other one went down and down and ended up a criminal. One day the criminal appeared before the judge. He had committed a crime to which he pleaded guilty. The judge recognised his old friend, and faced a dilemma. He was a judge so he had to be just; he couldn't let the man off. On the other hand, he didn't want to punish the man, because he loved him. So he told his friend that he would fine him the correct penalty for the offence. That is justice. Then he came down from his position as judge and he wrote a cheque for the amount of the fine. He gave it to his friend, saying that he would pay the penalty for him. That is love.

This is an illustration of what God has done for us. In his justice, he judges us because we are guilty, but then, in his love, he came down in the person of his Son Jesus Christ and paid the penalty for us. In this way he is both 'just' (in that he does not allow the guilty to go unpunished) and 'the one who justifies' – Romans 3:26 (in that by taking the penalty himself, in the person of his Son, he enables us to go free). He is both our Judge and our Saviour. It is not an innocent third party but God himself who saves us. In effect, he gives us a cheque and says we have a choice: do we want him to pay it for us or are we going to face the judgement of God for our own wrong-doing?

The illustration I have used is not an exact one for three reasons. First, our plight is worse. The penalty we are facing is not just a fine, but death. Secondly, the relationship is closer. This is not just two friends: it is our Father in heaven who loves us more than any earthly parent loves their own child. Thirdly, the cost was greater: it cost God not money, but his one and only Son – who paid *the penalty of sin*.

The fourth image comes from *the home*. We saw that both the root and the result of sin were a broken relationship with God. The result of the cross is the possibility of a restored relationship with God. Paul says that '*God was* reconciling the world to himself *in Christ*' (2 Corinthians 5:19, italics mine). Some people caricature the New Testament teaching and suggest that God is unjust because he punished Jesus, an innocent party, instead of us. This is not what the New Testament says. Rather, Paul says, 'God was . . . in Christ.' He was himself the substitute in the person of his Son. He made it possible for us to be restored to a relationship with him. The *partition of sin* has been destroyed. What happened to the Prodigal Son can happen to us. We can come back to the Father and experience his love and blessing. The relationship is not only for this life: it is eternal. One day we will be with the Father in heaven – there we will be free, not only from the penalty of sin, the power of sin, the pollution of sin and the partition of sin, but also from the presence of sin. That is what God has made possible through his self-substitution on the cross.

God loves each one of us so much and longs to be in a relationship with us as a human parent longs to be in a relationship with each of their children. It is not just that Jesus died for everyone. He died for you and for me; it is very personal. Paul writes of 'the Son of God, who loved me and gave himself for me' (Galatians 2:20). If you had been the only person in the world, Jesus would have died for you. Once we see the cross in these personal terms, our lives will be transformed.

John Wimber, an American pastor and church leader, described how the cross became a personal reality to him:

After I had studied the Bible . . . for about three months I could have passed an elementary exam on the cross. I understood there is one God who could be known in three Persons. I understood Jesus is fully God and fully man and he died on the cross for the sins of the world. But I didn't understand that I was a sinner. I thought I was a good guy. I knew I messed up here and there but I didn't realise how serious my condition was.

But one evening around this time Carol [his wife] said, 'I think it's time to do something about all that we've been learning.' Then, as I looked on in utter amazement, she knelt down on the floor and started praying to what seemed to me to be the ceiling plaster. 'Oh God,' she said, 'I am sorry for my sin.'

I couldn't believe it. Carol was a better person than I, yet she thought she was a sinner. I could feel her pain and the depth of her prayers. Soon she was weeping and repeating, 'I am sorry for my sin.' There were six or seven people in the room, all with their eyes closed. I looked at them and then it hit me: *They've all prayed this prayer too!* I started sweating bullets. I thought I was going to die. The perspiration ran down my face and I thought, 'I'm not going to do this. This is dumb. I'm a good guy.' Then it struck me. Carol wasn't praying to the plaster; she was praying to a person, to a God who could hear her. In comparison to him she knew she was a sinner in need of forgiveness.

In a flash the cross made personal sense to me. Suddenly I knew something that I had never known before; I had hurt God's feelings. He loved me and in his love for me he sent Jesus. But I had turned away from that love; I had shunned it all of my life. I was a sinner, desperately in need of the cross.

Then I too was kneeling on the floor, sobbing, nose running, eyes watering, every square inch of my flesh perspiring profusely. I had this overwhelming sense that I was talking with someone who had been with me all of my life, but whom I failed to recognise. Like Carol, I began talking to the living God, telling him that I was a sinner but the only words I could say aloud were, 'Oh God, Oh God.'

I knew something revolutionary was going on inside of me. I thought, 'I hope this works, because I'm making a complete fool of myself.' Then the Lord brought to mind a man I had seen in Pershing Square in Los Angeles a number of years before. He was wearing a sign that said, 'I'm a fool for Christ. Whose fool are you?' I thought at the time, 'That's the most stupid thing I've ever seen.' But as I kneeled on the floor I realised the truth of the odd sign: the cross is foolishness 'to those who are perishing' (1 Corinthians 1:18). That night I knelt at the cross and believed in Jesus. I've been a fool for Christ ever since.[28]

4

How Can We Have Faith?

At the age of eighteen in many ways life could not have been better. I was halfway through my first year at university. I was having fun and every opportunity of life seemed open to me. Christianity had no appeal for me; indeed the reverse. I felt that if I became a Christian, life would become very boring. I imagined God wanted to stop all the fun and make me do all sorts of tedious religious things.

On the other hand, as I looked at the evidence for Christianity, I became convinced it was true. I thought the answer was to delay the decision, enjoy life now and become a Christian on my death-bed. Yet I knew I could not do that with integrity. Very reluctantly I gave my life to Christ.

What I had failed to realise is that Christianity is about a relationship with God – a God who loves us and wants the very best for us. I was, to use the title of C. S. Lewis' book about his own experience of Christ, 'surprised by joy'. Becoming a Christian was the start of the most exciting relationship. Indeed, it was the start of a new life. As Paul wrote, 'those who become Christians become new persons. They are not the same any more for the old is gone. A new life has begun' (2 Corinthians 5:17, *The New Living Bible*). I sometimes keep a note of what people say or write after they have just started the new life that Paul is speaking about. Here are two examples:

> I now have hope where previously there was only despair. I can forgive now, where before there was only coldness . . . God is so alive for me. I can feel him guiding me and the complete and utter loneliness which I have been feeling is gone. God is filling a deep, deep void.

> I felt like hugging everybody in the street . . . I cannot stop praying, I even missed my bus stop today because I was so busy praying on the top deck.

Experiences vary greatly. Some immediately know a difference. For others it is more gradual. What matters is not so much the experience as the fact that when we receive Christ, we become a child of God. It is the start of a new relationship. As the Apostle John writes, 'Yet to all who received him, to those who believed in his name, he gave the right to become children of God' (John 1:12).

Good parents want their children to be sure about their

relationship with them. In the same way, God wants us to be sure about our relationship with him. Many people are uncertain about whether they are Christians or not. I ask people at the end of Alpha courses to fill in questionnaires. One of the questions I ask is, 'Would you have described yourself as a Christian at the beginning of the course?' Here is a list of some of the answers:

'Yes, but without any real experience of a relationship with God.'
'Sort of.'
'Possibly yes/think so.'
'Not sure.'
'Probably.'
'Ish.'
'Yes – though looking back possibly no.'
'No, a semi-Christian.'

The New Testament makes it clear that it is possible for us to be sure that we are Christians and that we have eternal life. The Apostle John writes, 'I write these things to you who believe in the name of the Son of God so that you may *know* that you have eternal life' (1 John 5:13, italics mine).

Just as three legs support a camera tripod, our assurance of our relationship with God stands firmly based on the activity of all three members of the Trinity: the promises which the Father gives us in his word, the sacrifice of the Son for us on the cross and the assurance of the Spirit in our hearts. These can be summarised under three headings: the word of God, the work of Jesus and the witness of the Holy Spirit.

THE WORD OF GOD

If we were to rely only on our feelings we could never be sure about anything. Our feelings go up and down depending on all sorts of factors, such as the weather or what we have had for breakfast.

They can be changeable and even deceptive. The promises in the Bible, which is the word of God, do not change and are totally reliable.

There are many great promises in the Bible. A verse which I found helpful, especially at the beginning of my Christian life, is one which comes in the last book of the Bible. In a vision John sees Jesus speaking to seven different churches. To the church in Laodicea Jesus says: 'Here I am! I stand at the door and knock. If anyone hears my voice and opens the door, I will come in and eat with them, and they with me' (Revelation 3:20).

There are many ways of speaking about starting the new life of the Christian faith – 'becoming a Christian', 'giving our lives to Christ', 'receiving Christ', 'inviting Jesus into our lives', 'believing in him' and 'opening the door to Jesus' are some of the variations. All of them describe the same reality; that Jesus enters our lives by the Holy Spirit, as is pictured in this verse.

The Pre-Raphaelite artist, Holman Hunt (1827-1910), inspired by this verse painted *The Light of the World*. He painted three versions in all. One hangs in Keble College, Oxford; another version is in the Manchester City Art Gallery; the most famous toured the colonies in 1905-7 and was presented to St Paul's Cathedral in June 1908, where it still hangs. When the first version was shown it received generally poor reviews. Then, on 5 May 1854, John Ruskin, the artist and critic, wrote to *The Times* and explained the symbolism at length and brilliantly defended it as 'one of the very noblest works of sacred art ever produced in this or any other age'.

Jesus, the Light of the World, stands at a door, which is overgrown with ivy and weeds. The door clearly represents the door of someone's life. This person has never invited Jesus to come into his or her life. Jesus is standing at the door and knocking. He is awaiting a response. He wants to come in and be part of that person's life. Apparently, someone said to Holman Hunt that he had made a mistake. They told him, 'You have forgotten to paint a handle on the door.'

'Oh no,' replied Hunt, 'that is deliberate. There is only one handle and that is on the inside.'

In other words, we have to open the door to let Jesus into our lives. Jesus will never force his way in. He gives us the freedom to choose. It is up to us whether or not we open the door to him. If we do, he promises, 'I will come in and eat with them and they with me.' Eating together is a sign of the friendship which Jesus offers to all those who open the door of their lives to him.

Once we have invited Jesus to come in, he promises that he will never leave us. He says to his disciples, 'I am with you always' (Matthew 28:20). We may not always be in direct conversation with him, but he will always be there. If you are working in a room with a friend, you may not be talking to each other all the time, but you are nevertheless aware of each other's presence. This is how it is with the presence of Jesus. He is with us always.

This promise of the presence of Jesus with us is closely related to another marvellous promise which comes in the New Testament. Jesus promises to give his followers eternal life (John 10:28). As we have seen, 'eternal life' in the New Testament is a quality of life which comes from living in a relationship with God through Jesus Christ (John 17:3). It starts now, when we experience the fullness of life which Jesus came to bring (John 10:10). Yet it is not just in this life; it goes on into eternity.

The resurrection of Jesus from the dead has many implications. First, it assures us about the past, that what Jesus achieved on the cross was effective. 'The resurrection is not the reversal of a defeat, but the proclamation of a victory.'[29] Secondly, it assures us about the present. Jesus is alive. His power is with us, bringing us life in all its fullness. Thirdly, it assures us about the future. This life is not the end; there is life beyond the grave. History is not meaningless or cyclical; it is moving towards a glorious climax.

One day Jesus will return to earth to establish a new heaven and a new earth (Revelation 21:1). Then those who are in Christ will go to 'be with the Lord for ever' (1 Thessalonians 4:17). There will be no more crying, for there will be no more pain. There will be no more temptation, for there will be no more sin. There will be no more suffering and no more separation from loved ones. Then we will see Jesus face to face (1 Corinthians 13:12). We will be given glorious and painless resurrection bodies (1 Corinthians 15). We will be transformed into the moral likeness of Jesus Christ (1 John 3:2). Heaven will be a place of intense joy and delight which goes on for ever. Some have ridiculed this by suggesting it would be monotonous or boring. But: 'No eye has seen, no ear has heard, no mind has conceived what God has prepared for those who love him' (1 Corinthians 2:9 quoting Isaiah 64:4).

As C. S. Lewis put it in one of his Narnia books:

The term is over: the holidays have begun. The dream is ended: this is the morning . . . all their life in this world . . . had only been the cover and the title page: now at last they were beginning Chapter One of the Great Story which no one on earth has read: which goes on forever: in which every chapter is better than the one before.[30]

THE WORK OF JESUS

When I was at university, I came across a book called *Heaven, Here I Come*. At first I, like many today, thought this was an arrogant claim. It *would* be arrogant to be so confident if it depended on us. If my entry into heaven depended on how good a life I'd led I would not have any hope of getting in at all.

The wonderful news is that it does not depend on me. It

depends on what Jesus has done for me. It depends not on what I do or achieve, but on his work on the cross. What he did on the cross enables him to give us eternal life as a gift (John 10:28; Romans 6:23b). We do not earn a gift. We accept it with gratitude.

Although eternal life is free, it is not cheap. It cost Jesus his life. We receive the gift by repentance and faith. The word for 'repentance' means changing our minds. If we want to receive this gift, we have to be willing to turn our backs on everything we know to be wrong. These are the things which do us harm and lead to 'death' (Romans 6:23a). Turning away from them is what the Bible calls repentance (literally changing our minds). C. S. Lewis describes it like this: 'Laying down your arms, surrendering, saying you are sorry, realising that you have been on the wrong track and being ready to start life over again from the ground floor – that is the only way out of this hole.'

What is faith? John Patton (1824-1907), a Scot from Dumfriesshire, travelled to the New Hebrides (a group of islands in the South-West Pacific) to tell the tribal people about Jesus. The islanders were cannibals and his life was in constant danger. Patton decided to work on a translation of John's Gospel, but found that there was no word in their language for 'belief' or 'trust'. Nobody trusted anybody else. Eventually, Patton hit upon a way to find the word he was looking for. One day, when his native servant came in, Patton raised both feet off the floor, sat back in his chair and asked, 'What am I doing now?' In reply, the servant used a word which means 'to lean your whole weight upon'. This was the expression Patton used. Faith is leaning our whole weight upon Jesus and what he has done for us on the cross.

Jean-Francois Gravelet (1824-1897), better known as Blondin, was a famous tightrope walker and acrobat. He was perhaps best known for his many crossings of a tightrope 1,100 feet (335 m) in length suspended 160 feet (50 m) above the Niagara Falls. His act would be watched by large crowds and began with a relatively simple crossing using a balancing pole. Then he would throw the pole away and begin to amaze the onlookers. On one occasion in 1860, a Royal party from Britain went to watch Blondin perform. He crossed the tightrope on stilts, then blindfolded; next he stopped halfway to cook and eat an omelette. He then wheeled a wheelbarrow from one side to the other as the crowd cheered. He put a sack of potatoes into the wheelbarrow and wheeled that across. The crowd cheered louder. Then he approached the Royal party and asked the Duke of Newcastle, 'Do you believe that I could take a man across the tightrope in this wheelbarrow?'

'Yes, I do,' said the Duke.

'Hop in!' replied Blondin. The crowd fell silent, but the Duke of Newcastle would not accept Blondin's challenge.

'Is there anyone else here who believes I could do it?' asked Blondin. No one was willing to volunteer. Eventually, an old woman stepped out of the crowd and climbed into the wheelbarrow. Blondin wheeled her all the way across and all the way back. The old woman was Blondin's mother, the only person willing to put her life in his hands. Faith is not merely intellectual, it involves an active step of putting our trust in Jesus.

If we accept God's gift, we cannot be secretive about it. We have to be ready to be known as Christians (Romans 10:9-10) and to identify with the people of God (Hebrews 11:25). It is not that we earn our salvation by our repentance, faith and public acceptance, but these are the means by which we accept the free gift. It was earned not by us, but by Jesus.

It all starts with God's love for us: 'For God so loved the world that he gave his one and only Son, that whoever believes in him shall not perish but have eternal life' (John 3:16). We all deserve to 'perish'. God, in his love for us, saw the mess we were in and gave his only Son, Jesus, to die for us. As a result of his death, everlasting life is offered to all who believe.

On the cross, Jesus took all our wrong-doing upon himself. This had been clearly prophesied in the Old Testament. In the Book of Isaiah, written hundreds of years beforehand, the prophet foresaw what 'the suffering servant' would do for us and said: 'We all, like sheep, have gone astray, each of us has turned to our own way; and the Lord has laid on him [ie, Jesus] the iniquity of us all' (Isaiah 53:6).

What the prophet is saying is that we have all done wrong – we have all gone astray. He says elsewhere that the things which we do wrong cause a separation between us and God (Isaiah 59:1-2). This is one of the reasons why God can seem remote. There is a barrier between us and him which prevents us from experiencing his love.

On the other hand, Jesus never did anything wrong. He lived a perfect life. There was no barrier between him and his Father. On the cross, God transferred our wrong-doings ('our iniquity') onto Jesus ('the Lord has laid on him the iniquity of us all'). That is why Jesus cried out on the cross, 'My God, my God, why have you forsaken me?' (Mark 15:34). At that moment he was cut off from God – not because of his own wrong-doing, but because of ours.

This made it possible for the barrier between us and God to be removed – for all who accept for themselves what Jesus has done for them. As a result, we can be sure of God's forgiveness. Our guilt has been taken away. We can be sure that we will never be condemned. As Paul puts it, 'Therefore, there is now no condemnation for those who are in Christ Jesus' (Romans 8:1). This, then, is the second reason we can be sure that we have eternal life – because of what Jesus achieved for us on the cross by dying for us.

THE WITNESS OF THE SPIRIT

When someone becomes a Christian, God's Holy Spirit comes to live within them. There are two aspects in particular of the many activities of the Holy Spirit which help us to be sure of our faith in Christ.

First, he transforms us from within. He produces the character of Jesus in our lives. This is called 'the fruit of the Spirit' – 'love, joy, peace, patience, kindness, goodness, faithfulness, gentleness and self-control' (Galatians 5:22-23). When the Holy Spirit comes to live within us this 'fruit' begins to grow.

There will be changes in our character which should be observable by other people, but obviously these changes do not occur overnight. We have just planted a pear tree in our garden and almost every day I look to see if it has any fruit. One day a friend of mine (the illustrator of this book) played a practical joke on me. He hung a large Granny Smith apple on the tree with cotton. Even I was not fooled by this. My limited knowledge of gardening tells me that fruit takes time to grow (and pear trees do not produce apples). We hope that over a period of time other people will notice that we are more loving, more joyful, more peaceful, more patient, more kind and more self-controlled.

As well as changes in our character there should be changes in our relationships – both with God and with other people. We develop a new love for God – Father, Son and Holy Spirit. For example, hearing the word 'Jesus' has a different emotional impact. Before I was a Christian, if I was listening to the radio or watching television and heard the subject change to Jesus Christ, I would probably have turned it off. After I became a Christian, I would turn it up, because my attitude to him had totally changed. This was a little sign of my new love for him.

Our attitude to others also changes. Often new Christians say to me that they are suddenly noticing the faces of people in the street and on the bus. Before they had little interest; now they feel a concern for people who often look sad and lost. I found that one of the biggest differences was in my attitude to other Christians. I am afraid that beforehand I had tended to avoid anyone who had a Christian faith. Afterwards, I found they weren't as bad as I had expected! Indeed, I soon started to experience a depth of friendship with other Christians which I had never known in my life before.

Secondly, as well as these changes which can be observed in our lives, the Holy Spirit also brings an inner experience of God. He creates a deep, personal conviction that we are children of God (Romans 8:15-16). This experience is different for everyone.

I have three children. To my mind, so many children are over-worked during their schooldays! The main advice I give them is, 'Don't work so hard!' Whatever is said in my children's school reports, I think they are fantastic. I remember looking at my thirteen-year-old daughter's report, which I (of course) thought was wonderful. She, however, was pointing out areas in which she was disappointed, and was saying that she should have done better in French, and so on. I kept responding, 'I don't really care how you did in French. I think you're fantastic. In fact, I wouldn't really care if your whole report was bad, I love you because I love you.'

As I was saying this, I suddenly sensed God saying, 'This is how I feel about you.' The love of God for each one of us is far greater than the love of human parents for their children. I am always feeling that I could do better, that I am not good at one thing or another, that I fail again and again. Yet God accepts us and loves us simply because he loves us. That is an example of the witness of the Spirit, the third way in which we are assured of our relationship with God, and that we are forgiven and have eternal life. We know it because the Spirit of God witnesses to us – both objectively through an ongoing change in our character and in our relationships, and subjectively through a deep inner conviction that we are children of God.

In these ways (the word of God, the work of Jesus and the witness of the Spirit), those who believe in Jesus can be sure that they are children of God and that they have eternal life.

It is not arrogant to be sure. It is based on what God has promised, on what Jesus died to achieve, and on the work of the Holy Spirit in our lives. It is one of the privileges of being a child of God that we can be absolutely confident about our relationship with our Father, that we can know his forgiveness and be sure that we are Christians and that we have eternal life.

If you are unsure about whether you have ever really believed in Jesus, here is a prayer which you can pray as a way of starting the Christian life and receiving all the benefits which Christ died to make possible.

> Heavenly Father, I am sorry for the things I have done wrong in my life. [Take a few moments to ask his forgiveness for anything particular that is on your conscience.] Please forgive me. I now turn from everything which I know is wrong.
>
> Thank you that you sent your Son, Jesus, to die on the cross for me so that I could be forgiven and set free. From now on I will follow and obey him as my Lord.

Thank you that you now offer me this gift of forgiveness and your Spirit. I now receive that gift.

Please come into my life by your Holy Spirit to be with me for ever. Through Jesus Christ, our Lord. Amen.

5

Why and How Do I Pray?

Surveys have shown that three-quarters of the population of sceptical, secular Britain admit to praying at least once a week. Before I became a Christian I prayed two different types of prayers. First, I prayed a prayer taught me as a child by my grandmother (who was not herself a churchgoer), 'God bless Mummy and Daddy . . . and everybody and make me a good boy. Amen.' There was nothing wrong with the prayer, but for me it was only a formula which I prayed every night before I went to sleep, with superstitious fears about what might go wrong if I didn't.

Secondly, I prayed in times of crisis. For example, at the age of seventeen I was travelling by myself in the USA. The bus company managed to lose my rucksack which contained my clothes, money and address book. I was left with virtually nothing. I spent ten days living on a hippie colony in Key West, sharing a tent with an alcoholic. After that, with a feeling of mounting loneliness and desperation, I spent the days wandering around various American cities and the nights on the bus. One day as I walked along the street, I cried out to God (in whom I did not believe) and prayed that I would meet someone I knew. Not long afterwards, I got on the bus at 6 am in Phoenix, Arizona, and there I saw an old school friend. He lent me some money and we travelled together for a few days. It made all the difference. I did not see it as an answer to prayer; only as a coincidence. Since becoming a Christian I have found that it is remarkable how many coincidences happen when we pray.

WHAT IS PRAYER?

Prayer is the most important activity of our lives. It is the main way in which we develop a relationship with our Father in heaven. Jesus said, 'When you pray, go into your room, close the door and pray to your Father, who is unseen' (Matthew 6:6). It is a relationship rather than a ritual. It is not a torrent of mechanical and mindless words. Jesus said, 'Do not keep on babbling like pagans' (Matthew 6:7). It is a conversation with our Father in heaven; a vertical conversation, not a horizontal one. A little boy once yelled, 'Please, God, bring me a big box of chocolates for my birthday.' To which his mother answered, 'There is no need to shout, dear! God isn't deaf.' Back came the reply, 'No, but Grandpa is, and he is in the next room!' When we pray, it is not to others, or to ourselves, but to God. So prayer is a matter of relationships and when we pray the whole Trinity is involved.

Christian prayer is prayer 'to your Father'

Jesus taught us to pray, 'Our Father in heaven' (Matthew 6:9). God is personal. Of course he is 'beyond personality' as C. S. Lewis put it, but he is nevertheless personal. All human beings are made in the image of God. Personhood is a reflection of something within the nature of God. He is our loving Father and we have the extra-ordinary privilege of being able to come into his presence and call him 'Abba' – the Aramaic word for which the nearest translation is 'Daddy' or 'Dear Father'. There is a remarkable intimacy about our relationship with God and about praying to our Father in heaven.

He is not only 'our Father'; he is 'our Father in heaven'. He has heavenly power. When we pray we are speaking to the Creator of the universe. On 20 August 1977, Voyager II, the inter-planetary probe launched to observe and transmit to earth data about the outer planetary system, set off from earth travelling faster than the speed of a bullet (90,000 miles per hour). On 28 August 1989 it reached planet Neptune, 2,700 million miles from the earth. Voyager II then left the solar system. It will not come within one light year of any star for 958,000 years. In our galaxy there are 100,000 million stars, like our sun. Our galaxy is one of 100,000 million galaxies. In a throwaway line in Genesis, the writer tells us, 'He also made the stars' (Genesis 1:16). Such is his power. Andrew Murray, the Christian writer, once said, 'The power of prayer depends almost entirely upon our apprehension of who it is with whom we speak.'

When we pray, we are speaking to a God who is both transcendent and immanent. He is far greater and more powerful than the universe which he created and yet he is there with us when we pray.

Christian prayer is through the 'Son'
Paul says that 'through him [Jesus] we both [Jews and Gentiles] have access to the Father by one Spirit' (Ephesians 2:18). Jesus said that his Father would give 'whatever you ask in my name' (John 15:16). We have no right in ourselves to come to God but we are able to do so 'through Jesus' and 'in his name'. That is why it is customary to end prayers with 'through Jesus Christ our Lord' or 'in the name of Jesus'. This is not just a formula; it is our acknowledgement of the fact that we can only come to God through Jesus.

It is Jesus, through his death on the cross, who removed the barrier between us and God. He is our great High Priest. That is why there is such power in the name of Jesus.

The value of a cheque depends not only on the amount, but also on the name that appears at the bottom. If I wrote out a cheque for ten million pounds it would be worthless; but if Bill Gates, reputed to be the richest man in the world, were to write a cheque for ten million pounds it would be worth exactly that. When we go to the bank of heaven, we have nothing deposited there. If I go in my own name I can achieve nothing; but Jesus Christ has unlimited credit in heaven. He has given us the privilege of using his name.

Christian prayer is prayer 'by one Spirit' (Ephesians 2:18)
We find it hard to pray, but God has not left us alone. He has given us his Spirit to live within us and help us to pray. Paul writes, 'In the same way, the Spirit helps us in our weakness. We do not know what we ought to pray, but the Spirit himself intercedes for us with groans that words cannot express. And he who searches our hearts knows the mind of the Spirit, because the Spirit intercedes for the saints in accordance with God's will' (Romans 8:26-27). In a later chapter we shall look in more detail at the work of the Spirit. Here, it is sufficient to note that when we pray, God is praying through us by his Spirit who lives in us as Christians.

WHY PRAY?

Prayer is a vital activity. There are many reasons for praying. In the first place it is the way in which we develop a relationship with our Father in heaven. Sometimes people say, 'God knows our needs, so why do we have to ask?' Well, it would not be much of a relationship if there was no communication. Of course, asking is not the only way in which we communicate with God. There are other forms of prayer: thanksgiving, praise, adoration, confession, listening, etc. But asking is an important part. As we ask God for things and see our prayers answered, our relationship with him grows.

Next, Jesus prayed and taught us to do the same. Jesus had an uninterrupted relationship with his Father. His life was one of constant prayer. There are numerous references to his praying (eg, Mark 1:35; Luke 6:12). He assumed his disciples would pray. He said, 'When you pray' (Matthew 6:7) not, '*If* you pray.'

Then again, if we need any further incentive, Jesus taught us that there are rewards for prayer (Matthew 6:6).

> The hidden rewards of prayer are too many to enumerate. In the words of the apostle Paul, when we cry, 'Abba, Father,' the Holy Spirit witnesses with our spirit that we are indeed God's children, and we are granted a strong assurance of his fatherhood and love. He lifts the light of his face upon us and gives us his peace. He refreshes our soul, satisfies our hunger, quenches our thirst. We know we are no longer orphans for the Father has adopted us; no longer prodigals for we have been forgiven; no longer alienated, for we have come home.[31]

Finally, prayer not only changes us but it also changes situations. Many people can accept that prayer will have a beneficial effect on themselves, but some have philosophical objections to the concept that prayer can change events and third parties. Rabbi Daniel Cohn-Scherbok of Kent University once wrote an article arguing that as God already knows the future it therefore must be fixed. To this Clifford Longley, the Religious Affairs correspondent of *The Times*, correctly replied, 'If God lives in the eternal present, he hears all prayers simultaneously. Therefore he can appropriate a prayer from next week, and attach it to an event a month ago. Prayers said after the event can be heard before they are spoken and taken into account before the event.' Or, to put it another way, God has all eternity to answer the split-second prayer of a driver who is about to crash.

On numerous occasions Jesus encouraged us to ask. He said, 'Ask and it will be given to you; seek and you will find; knock and the door will be opened to you. For everyone who asks receives; everyone who seeks finds; and to everyone who knocks, the door will be opened' (Matthew 7:7-8).

Every Christian knows, through experience, that God answers prayer. It is not possible to prove Christianity on the basis of answers to prayer because they can always be explained away by cynics as coincidences. But the cumulative effective of answered prayer reinforces our faith in God. I keep a prayer diary and it is fascinating to me to see how day after day, week after week, year after year, God has answered my prayers.

DOES GOD ALWAYS ANSWER PRAYER?

In the passage I have cited from Matthew 7:7-8 and in many other New Testament passages the promises appear to be absolute. However, when we look at the whole of Scripture, we see there are good reasons why we may not always get what we ask for.

Unconfessed sin causes a barrier between us and God: 'Surely the arm of the Lord is not too short to save, nor his ear too dull to hear. But your iniquities have separated you from your God; your sins have hidden his face from you, so that he will not hear' (Isaiah 59:1-2). God never promises to answer the prayer of a person who is not living in a relationship with him. Sometimes, he may graciously answer the prayer of an unbeliever (as he did in the example I gave at the beginning of the chapter), but we have no right to expect it. When people say, 'I don't feel I am getting through to God. I don't feel there is anyone there,' the first question to ask them is whether they have ever received God's forgiveness through Christ on the cross. The barrier must be removed before we can expect God to hear and answer our prayers.

Even as Christians our friendship with God can be marred by sin or disobedience. John writes, 'Dear friends, if our hearts do not condemn us, we have confidence before God and receive from him anything we ask, because we obey his commands and do what pleases him' (1 John 3:21-22). If we are conscious of any sin or disobedience towards God, we need to confess it and turn from it so that our friendship with God can be restored and we can approach him again with confidence.

Our motivation can also be a hindrance to getting what we ask for. Not every request for a new Porsche gets answered! James, the brother of Jesus, writes:

> You want something but don't get it. You kill and covet, but you cannot have what you want. You quarrel and fight. You do not have, because you do not ask God. When you ask, you do not receive, because you ask with wrong motives, that you may spend what you get on your pleasures (James 4:2-3).

A famous example of a prayer riddled with wrong motives is that of John Ward of Hackney, written in the eighteenth century:

> O Lord, thou knowest that I have nine estates in the City of London, and likewise that I have lately purchased one estate in fee simple in the county of Essex; I beseech thee to preserve the two counties of Essex and Middlesex from fire and earthquake; and as I have a mortgage in Hertfordshire, I beg of thee likewise to have an eye of compassion on that county; and for the rest of the counties thou mayest deal with them as thou art pleased.
>
> O Lord, enable the bank to answer their bills, and make all my debtors good men. Give a prosperous voyage and return to the Mermaid ship, because I have insured it; and as thou hast said that the days of the wicked are but short, I trust in thee, that thou wilt not forget thy promise, as I have purchased an estate in reversion which will be mine on the death of that profligate young man, Sir J. L.
>
> Keep my friends from sinking, and preserve me from thieves and house breakers, and make all my servants so honest and faithful that they may attend to my interests, and never cheat me out of my property, night or day.

We see here why the promises in the Bible that prayers will be answered are sometimes qualified. For example, John writes, 'If we ask anything *according to his will*, he hears us' (1 John 5:14, italics mine). The more we get to know God, the better we will know his will and the more our prayers will be answered.

Sometimes prayers are not answered because what we are requesting is not good for us. God only promises to give us 'good gifts' (Matthew 7:11). He loves us and knows what is best for us. Good parents do not always give their children what they ask for. If a five-year-old wants to play with a carving knife, hopefully a good parent will say 'no'! God will answer 'no' if the things we ask for are 'either not good in themselves, or not good for us or for others, directly or indirectly, immediately or ultimately', as John Stott has written.

The answer to our prayer will either be 'yes', 'no' or sometimes 'wait', and for this we should be extremely grateful. If we were given carte blanche we would never dare pray again. As the preacher Martyn Lloyd-Jones put it, 'I thank God that he is not prepared to do anything that I may chance to ask him . . . I am profoundly grateful to God that he did not grant me certain things for which I asked, and that he shut certain doors in my face.'[32] Any Christian who has been a Christian for some time will appreciate this sentiment. Ruth Graham (married to Billy Graham) told an audience in Minneapolis, 'God has not always answered my prayers. If he had, I would have married the wrong man – several times.' Sometimes we will not know during this life why the answer was 'no'. I can think of an occasion in 1996 when I was playing squash with one of my closest friends, Mick Hawkins, a man of forty-two with six children. In the middle of the game he dropped dead from a heart attack. I have never cried out to God more than I did on that occasion; asking him to heal him, restore him, praying that the heart attack would not be fatal. I do not know why he died.

I remember early the following morning – obviously I could not sleep – I went out for a walk and said to the Lord, 'I don't understand why Mick died. He was such an amazing person, such a wonderful husband and father. I don't understand . . .' Then I realised I had a choice. I could say, 'I am going to stop believing.' The alternative was to say, 'I am going to go on believing in spite of the fact that I don't understand and I am going to trust you, Lord, even though I don't think I will ever understand – in this life – why it happened.'

There may be times when we will have to wait until we meet God face to face to understand what his will was and why our prayer did not get the answer we hoped for.

HOW SHOULD WE PRAY?

There is no set way to pray. Prayer is an integral part of our relationship with God and therefore we are free to talk to him as we wish. God does not want us to repeat meaningless words; he wants to hear what is on our hearts. Having said that, many people find it helpful to have a pattern for prayer. For some years I used the mnemonic ACTS.

- **A** – adoration – praising God for who he is and what he has done.
- **C** – confession – asking God's forgiveness for anything that we have done wrong.
- **T** – thanksgiving – for health, family, friends, and so on.
- **S** – supplication – praying for ourselves, for our friends, and for others.

More recently I have found that I often follow the pattern from the Lord's Prayer (Matthew 6:9-13):

'Our Father in heaven' (v. 9)
We have already looked earlier in the chapter at what this phrase means. Under this heading, I spend time thanking God for who he is and for my relationship with him and for the ways in which he has answered prayers.

'Hallowed be your name' (v. 9)
In Hebrew someone's name signified a revelation of that person's character. To pray that God's name be hallowed is to pray that he will be honoured. So often we look around our society and see that God's name is dishonoured – many people pay no attention to him or his laws. We should start by praying that God's name is honoured in our own lives, in our church and in the society around us.

'Your kingdom come' (v. 10)

God's kingdom is his rule and reign. That will be complete when Jesus comes again. But this kingdom broke into history when Jesus came for the first time. Jesus demonstrated this presence of God's kingdom in his own ministry. When we pray, 'Your kingdom come,' we are praying for God's rule and reign to come both in the future and in the present. It includes praying for people to be converted, healed, set free from evil, filled with the Spirit and given the gifts of the Spirit, in order that we may together serve and obey the King.

I am told that D. L. Moody wrote down a list of 100 people and prayed for them to be converted in his lifetime. Ninety-six of them were converted by the time he died and the other four were converted at his funeral.

One Christian mother was having problems with her rebellious teenage son. He was lazy, bad-tempered, a cheat, a liar and a thief. Later on, though outwardly respected as a lawyer, his life was dominated by worldly ambition and a desire to make money. His morals were loose. He lived with several different women and had a son by one of them. At one stage he joined a weird religious sect and adopted all kinds of strange practices. Throughout this time his mother continued to pray for him. One day, the Lord gave her a vision and she wept as she prayed, because she saw the light of Jesus Christ in him, and his face transformed. She had to wait another nine years before her son gave his life to Jesus Christ at the age of thirty-two. That man's name was Augustine. He went on to become one of the greatest theologians in the church. He always attributed his conversion to the prayers of his mother.

We are praying not simply for God's rule and reign in individuals' lives but ultimately for the transformation of society. We are praying for God's peace, justice and compassion. We are praying for those often marginalised by society but for whom God cares especially, such as widows, orphans, the lonely and prisoners (Psalm 68:4-6a).

'Your will be done on earth as it is in heaven' (v. 10)

This is not resignation, it is a releasing of the burdens that we so often carry. Many people are worried about decisions they are facing. The decisions may be about major or minor issues but if we want to be sure that we don't make a mistake we need to pray, 'Your will be done.' The psalmist says, 'Commit your way to the Lord; trust in him and he will act' (Psalm 37:5, RSV). For example, if you are praying about whether a relationship is right, you might pray, 'If this relationship is wrong, I pray that you stop it. If it is right I pray that nothing will stop it.' Then, having committed it to the Lord, you can trust him and wait for him to act. (We will look at this subject in more detail in Chapter 7 – and the principles in that chapter need to be taken into account.)

'Give us today our daily bread' (v. 11)

Some have suggested that Jesus meant the spiritual bread of Holy Communion or the Bible. This is possible, but I believe the reformers were right to say that Jesus is referring here to our basic needs. Luther said it indicated 'everything necessary for the preservation of this life, like food, a healthy body, good weather, house, home, wife, children, good government and peace'. God is concerned about everything that you and I are concerned about. Just as I want my children to talk about anything they are worried about, so God wants to hear about the things we are concerned about.

A friend of mine asked a new Christian how her small business was going. She replied that it was not going very well. So my friend offered to pray for it. The new Christian replied, 'I didn't know that was allowed.' My friend explained that it was. They prayed and the following week the business improved considerably. The Lord's Prayer teaches us that it is not wrong to pray about our own concerns, provided that God's name, God's kingdom and God's will are our first priority.

'Forgive us our debts, as we also have forgiven our debtors' (v. 12)
Jesus taught us to pray that God would forgive us our debts (ie, the things which we do wrong). Some say, 'Why do we need to pray for forgiveness? Surely when we come to the cross we are already forgiven for everything, past, present and future?' It is true, as we have seen in the chapter on why Jesus died, that we are totally forgiven for everything, past, present and future because Jesus took all our sins on himself on the cross. Yet Jesus still tells us to pray, 'Forgive us our debts.' I find the most helpful analogy is the one given by Jesus in John 13 when Jesus moves to wash Peter's feet. Peter said, 'No, you shall never wash my feet.' Jesus answered, 'Unless I wash you, you have no part of me.' Peter replied, in effect, 'Well, in that case wash my whole body.' Jesus said, 'A person who has had a bath needs only to wash his feet; his whole body is clean.' This is a picture of forgiveness. When we come to the cross we are made totally clean and we are forgiven – everything is dealt with. But as we go through the world we do things which tarnish our friendship with God. Our relationship is always secure but our friendship is sullied with the dirt that we pick up on our feet. Each day we need to pray, 'Lord forgive us, cleanse us from the dirt.' We don't need to have a bath again, Jesus has done that for us, but a measure of cleansing may be necessary every day.

Jesus went on to say, 'If you forgive others when they sin against you, your heavenly Father will also forgive you. But if you do not forgive others their sins, your Father will not forgive your sins' (Matthew 6:14-15). This does not mean that by forgiving people we can earn forgiveness. We can never earn forgiveness. Jesus achieved that for us on the cross. But the sign that we are forgiven is that we are willing to forgive other people. If we are not willing to forgive other people that is evidence that we do not know forgiveness ourselves. If we really know God's forgiveness, we cannot refuse forgiveness to someone else.

'Lead us not into temptation, but deliver us from the evil one' (v. 13)
God does not tempt us (James 1:13), but he is in control of how much we are exposed to the devil (eg, Job 1–2). Every Christian has a weak area – be it fear, selfish ambition, greed, pride, lust, gossiping, cynicism or something else. If we know our weakness, we can pray for protection against it, as well, of course, as taking action to avoid unnecessary temptation. We will consider this whole issue in Chapter 11.

WHEN SHOULD WE PRAY?

The New Testament exhorts us to pray 'always' (1 Thessalonians 5:17; Ephesians 6:18). We do not have to be in a special building in order to pray. We can pray on the tube, on the bus, in the car, on our bike, walking along the road, as we lie in bed, in the middle of the night, whenever and wherever we are. As in any close relationship, we can continue an ongoing conversation. Nevertheless, it is helpful to have time together when you know that you are meeting simply to talk. Jesus said, 'When you pray, go into your room, close the door and pray to your Father, who is unseen' (Matthew 6:6). He himself went off to a solitary place in order to pray (Mark 1:35). I find it helpful to combine Bible reading and prayer at the beginning of the day, when my mind is most active. It is good to have a regular pattern. What time of day we choose will depend on our circumstances and our own particular make-up.

As well as praying alone, it is important to pray with other people. This could be in a small group of two or three for example. Jesus said, 'I tell you that if two of you on earth agree about anything you ask for, it will be done for you by my Father in heaven' (Matthew 18:19). It can be very hard praying aloud in front of other people. I remember the first time I did this, about two months after I had come to Christ. I was with two of my closest friends and we decided that we would spend some time praying together. We only prayed for about ten minutes, but when I took my shirt off afterwards it was wringing wet! Nevertheless, it is worth persevering since there is great power in praying together (Acts 12:5).

Prayer is at the heart of Christianity, because at the heart of Christianity is a relationship with God. That is why it is the most important activity of our lives. As the saying goes:

> Satan laughs at our words.
> Mocks at our toil.
> But trembles when we pray.

6

Why and How Should I Read
the Bible?

It was Valentine's night 1974. I had been to a party and was sitting in my room at college when my greatest friend came back with his girlfriend (now his wife) and told me that they had become Christians. I was immediately alarmed about them, thinking that the Moonies had got them and they needed my help.

I was at times an atheist and at times an agnostic, unsure of what I believed. I had been baptised and confirmed, but it had not meant much to me. At school I had been to chapel regularly and studied the Bible in RE lessons. But I had ended up rejecting it all and, indeed, arguing powerfully (or so I thought) against Christianity.

Now I wanted to help my friends, so I thought I would embark on a thorough research of the subject. I made a plan to read the Koran, Karl Marx, Jean-Paul Sartre (the existentialist philosopher) and the Bible. I happened to have a rather dusty copy of the Bible on my shelves, so that night I picked it up and started reading. I read all the way through Matthew, Mark and Luke, and halfway through John's Gospel. Then I fell asleep. When I woke up, I finished John's Gospel and carried on through Acts, Romans, and

1 and 2 Corinthians. I was completely gripped by what I read. I had read it before and it had meant virtually nothing to me. This time it came alive and I could not put it down. It had a ring of truth about it. I knew as I read it that I had to respond because it spoke so powerfully to me. Very shortly afterwards I came to put my faith in Jesus Christ.

Since then the Bible has become a 'delight' to me. The psalmist says:

> Blessed are those who do not walk in the counsel of the wicked or stand in the way of sinners or sit in the seat of mockers. But their delight is in the law of the Lord, and on his law they meditate day and night. They are like trees planted by streams of water, which yield their fruit in season and whose leaves do not wither. Whatever they do prospers (Psalm 1:1-3).

I love that phrase, 'their delight is in the law of the Lord.' All the psalmist had at that stage was the first five books of the Bible. They were his delight. In this chapter I want to look at why and how the Bible can become a 'delight' for each of us, looking, by way of introduction, at its uniqueness.

First, it is uniquely popular. It is estimated that 44 million Bibles are sold a year and that there is an average of 6.8 Bibles in every American household. An article in *The Times* recently was subheaded 'Forget the modern British novelists and TV tie-ins; the Bible is the biggest-selling book every year'. The writer remarked:

> As usual the top seller by several miles was the . . . Bible. If cumulative sales of the Bible were frankly reflected in bestseller lists, it would be a rare week when anything else would achieve a look in. It is wonderful, weird, or just plain baffling in this increasingly godless age – when the range of books available grows wider with each passing year – that this one book should go on selling hand over fist, month in, month out. . . .

It is estimated that nearly 1,250,000 Bibles and Testaments are sold in the UK each year.

The writer ends by saying, '*All* versions of the Bible sell well *all* the time. Can the Bible Society offer an explanation? "Well," I am told disarmingly, "it is such a good book."'

Secondly, it is uniquely powerful. In May 1928, the Prime Minister Stanley Baldwin said, 'The Bible is a high explosive. But it works in strange ways and no living man can tell or know how

that book, in its journey through the world, has startled the individual soul in ten thousand different places into a new life, a new world, a new belief, a new conception, a new faith.'

In recent times there has been a rising interest in the occult. People play with ouija boards, see occult films, have their fortunes told and read horoscopes. They want to get in touch with the supernatural. The tragedy is that they are seeking to communicate with supernatural evil forces, whereas what God offers us in the Bible is an opportunity to meet with the supernatural powers of good. To meet with the living God is so much more thrilling, more satisfying and a great deal wiser.

Thirdly, it is uniquely precious. About sixteen years ago I was on holiday with my family in central Asia, part of the USSR as it then was. At that time Bibles were strictly illegal there, but I took some Christian literature, including some Russian Bibles. While I was there I went to churches and looked for people who seemed from their faces to be genuine Christians. (At that time the meetings were usually infiltrated by the KGB.) On one occasion I followed a man, who was probably in his sixties, down the street after a service. I went up to him and tapped him on the shoulder. There was nobody about. I took out one of my Bibles and handed it to him. For a moment he had an expression of almost disbelief. Then he took from his pocket a New Testament which was probably 100 years old. The pages were so threadbare they were virtually transparent. When he realised that he had received a whole Bible, he was elated. He didn't speak any English and I didn't speak any Russian. We hugged each other and he started to run down the street jumping for joy, because he knew that the Bible was the most precious thing in the world.

Why is it so popular, so powerful and so precious? Jesus said: 'People do not live on bread alone, but on every word that comes from the mouth of God' (Matthew 4:4). The word is in the present tense, and means 'is continually coming out of the mouth of God'; it is like a stream pouring forth and, like the stream of a fountain, is never static. God is continually wanting to communicate with his people. He does so, primarily, through the Bible.

A MANUAL FOR LIFE – GOD HAS SPOKEN

God has spoken to us through his Son, Jesus Christ (Hebrews 1:2). Christianity is a revealed faith. We cannot find out about God unless God reveals himself. God has revealed himself in a person, Jesus Christ. He is God's ultimate revelation.

The main way we know about Jesus is through God's revelation recorded in the Bible. Biblical theology should be the study of God's revelation in the Bible. God has also revealed himself through creation (Romans 1:19-20; Psalm 19). Science is an exploration of God's revelation in creation. (There should be no conflict between science and the Christian faith; rather they complement one another.) God also speaks to people directly by his Spirit: through prophecy, dreams, visions, and through other people. We will look at all these in more detail later – especially in the chapter on guidance. In this chapter we will look at the way in which God speaks through the Bible.

Paul wrote of the inspiration of the Scriptures that were available to him: 'All Scripture is God-breathed and is useful for teaching, rebuking, correcting and training in righteousness, so that God's servant may be thoroughly equipped for every good work' (2 Timothy 3:16-17).

The word for 'God-breathed' is *theopneustos*. It is often translated as 'inspired by God'; but transliterated it is 'God-breathed'. The writer is saying that Scripture is God speaking. Of course he used human agents. It is 100 per cent the work of human beings. But it is also 100 per cent inspired by God (just as Jesus is fully human and fully God).

This is the way in which Jesus himself treated the Scriptures of his day. For him, what the Scriptures said, God said (Mark 7:5-13). If Jesus is our Lord, our attitude to the Scriptures should be the same as his. 'Belief in Christ as the supreme revelation of God leads to belief in scriptural inspiration – of the Old Testament by the direct testimony of Jesus and of the New Testament by inference from his testimony.'[33]

This high view of the inspiration of the Bible has been held almost universally by the worldwide church down the ages. The early theologians of the church had this view. Irenaeus (c. AD 130-200) said, 'The Scriptures are perfect.' Likewise, the reformers, for example Martin Luther, spoke of 'Scripture which has never erred'. Today, the Roman Catholic official view is enshrined in Vatican II. The Scriptures 'written under the inspiration of the Holy Spirit . . . have God as their author . . .'. Therefore they must be acknowledged as being 'without error'. This also, until the last century, was the view of all Protestant churches throughout the world, and although today it is questioned and even ridiculed at a school level, it continues to be held by many fine scholars.

This does not mean that there are no difficulties in the Bible. Even Peter found some of Paul's letters 'hard to understand' (2 Peter 3:16). There are moral and historical difficulties and some apparent contradictions. Some of the difficulties can be explained by the different contexts in which the authors were writing. It is important to remember that the Bible was written over a period of 1,500 years by at least forty authors, including kings, scholars, philosophers, fishermen, poets, statesmen, historians and doctors.

There is a whole range of genres: historical, narrative, poetry, prophecy, letters and apocalyptic literature.

Although some of the apparent contradictions can be explained by differing contexts, others are harder to resolve. This does not mean, however, that it is impossible and that we should abandon our belief in the inspiration of Scripture. Every great doctrine of the Christian faith has its difficulties. For example, it is hard to reconcile the love of God and the suffering in the world. Yet every Christian believes in the love of God and seeks an understanding of the problem of suffering within that framework. In a similar way we need to hold on to the belief in the inspiration of the Bible and try to understand the difficult passages within that context. It is important not to run away from the difficulties but to seek, so far as we can, to resolve them to our own satisfaction.

It is very important to hold on to the fact that *all* Scripture is inspired by God, even if we cannot immediately resolve all the difficulties. If we do, it should transform the way in which we live our lives. When Billy Graham was a young man several people (among them, one was called Chuck) started to say to him, 'You can't believe everything in the Bible.' He began to worry about it and started to become very muddled. John Pollock, in his biography of the evangelist, records what happened:

> So I went back and I got my Bible, and I went out in the moonlight. And I got to a stump and put the Bible on the stump, and I knelt down, and I said, 'Oh, God; I cannot prove certain things. I cannot answer some of the questions Chuck is raising and some of the other people are raising, but I accept this Book by faith as the Word of God.' I stayed by the stump praying wordlessly, my eyes moist . . . I had a tremendous sense of God's presence. I had a great peace that the decision I had made was right.[34]

If we accept that the Bible is inspired by God, then its authority must follow from that. If it is God's word then it must be our supreme authority for what we believe and how we act. For Jesus, it s supreme authority – above what the church leaders of his time said (eg, Mark 7:1-20) and above the opinions of others, however clever they were (eg, Mark 12:18-27). Having said that, we must of course give due weight to what church leaders and others say.

The Bible should be our authority in all matters of 'creed and conduct'. As we have seen, 'All Scripture is God-breathed and is useful for teaching, rebuking, correcting and training in righteousness' (2 Timothy 3:16). First, it is our authority for what we believe (our creed) – and therefore for 'teaching' and 'rebuking'. It is in the Bible that we find what God says (and what we should, therefore, believe) about suffering, about Jesus, about the cross, and so on.

Secondly, it is our authority for how we act (our conduct) – for 'correcting' and for 'training in righteousness'. It is here that we find out what is wrong in God's eyes and how we can live a righteous life. For instance, 'The ten commandments . . . are a brilliant analysis of the minimum conditions on which a society, a people, a nation can live a sober, righteous and civilised life.'[35]

There are some things that are very clear in the Bible. It tells us how to conduct our day-to-day lives, for example, when we're at work or under pressure. We know from the Bible that the single state can be a high calling (1 Corinthians 7:7), but it is the exception rather than the rule; marriage is the norm (Genesis 2:24; 1 Corinthians 7:2). We know that sexual intercourse outside marriage is wrong. We know that it is right to try to get a job if we can. We know it is right to give and to forgive. We are also given, among other things, guidelines on how to bring up our children and to care for elderly relatives.

Some people say, 'I don't want this rule book. It is too restrictive – all those rules and regulations. I want to be free. If you live by the Bible, you are not free to enjoy life.' But is that really right? Does the Bible take away our freedom? Or does it in fact give us freedom? Rules and regulations can in fact create freedom and increase enjoyment.

A few years ago, a football match had been arranged involving twenty-two small boys, including one of my sons, aged eight at the time. A friend of mine called Andy (who had been training the boys all year) was going to referee. Unfortunately, by 2.30 pm he had not turned up. The boys could wait no longer. I was press-ganged into being the substitute referee. There were a number of difficulties with this: I had no whistle; there were no markings for the boundaries of the pitch; I didn't know any of the other boys' names; they did not have colours to distinguish which sides they were on; and I did not know the rules nearly as well as some of the boys.

The game soon descended into complete chaos. Some shouted that the ball was in. Others said that it was out. I wasn't at all sure, so I let things run. Then the fouls started. Some cried, 'Foul!' Others said, 'No foul!' I didn't know who was right. So I let them play on. Then people began to get hurt. By the time Andy arrived, there were three boys lying injured on the ground and all the rest were shouting, mainly at me! But the moment Andy arrived, he blew his whistle, arranged the teams, told them where the boundaries were and had them under complete control. Then the boys had the game of their lives.

Were the boys more free without the rules or were they in fact less free? Without any effective authority they were free to do exactly what they wanted. The result was that people were confused and hurt. They much preferred it when they knew where the boundaries were. Then within those boundaries they were free to enjoy the game.

In some ways the Bible is like that. It is God's rule book. He tells us what is 'in' and what is 'out'. He tells us what we can do and what we must not do. If we play within the rules there is freedom and joy. When we break the rules, people get hurt. God did not say, 'Do not murder,' in order to ruin our enjoyment of life. He did not say, 'Do not commit adultery,' because he is a spoilsport. He did not want people to get hurt. When people leave their wives or husbands and children to commit adultery, lives get messed up.

The Bible is God's revelation of his will for his people. The more we discover his will and put it into practice, the freer we shall be. God has spoken. We need to hear what he has said.

A LOVE LETTER FROM GOD – GOD SPEAKS

For some people the Bible is never more than a well-thumbed manual for life. They believe God has spoken and they may study the Bible for hours. They analyse it, read commentaries on it (and there is nothing wrong with that), but they do not seem to realise that not only has God spoken, but he still speaks today through what he has said in the Bible. God's desire is that we should live in a relationship with him. He wants to speak to us daily through his word. So as well as being a manual for life, it is also a love letter.

The main point of the Bible is to show us how to enter into a relationship with God through Jesus Christ. Jesus said, 'You diligently study the Scriptures because you think that by them you possess eternal life. These are the Scriptures that testify about me, yet you refuse to come to me to have life' (John 5:39-40).

Dr Christopher Chavasse, formerly Bishop of Rochester, said:

The Bible is the portrait of our Lord Jesus Christ. The Gospels are the figure itself in the portrait. The Old Testament is the background leading up to the divine figure, pointing towards it and absolutely necessary to the composition as a whole. The Epistles serve as the dress and accoutrements of the figure, explaining and describing it. Then, while by our Bible reading we study the portrait as a great whole, the miracle happens, the figure comes to life and stepping down from the canvas of the written word, the everlasting Christ of the Emmaus story becomes himself our Bible teacher, to interpret to us in all the Scriptures the things concerning himself.

It is no good studying the Bible if we never come to Jesus Christ; if we never meet with him as we read it. Martin Luther said, 'Scripture is the manger or "cradle" in which the infant Jesus lies. Don't let us inspect the cradle and forget to worship the baby.'

Our relationship with God is two-way. We speak to him in prayer and he speaks to us in many ways, but especially through the Bible. God speaks through what he has spoken. The writer of the epistle to the Hebrews says, when he quotes the Old Testament, 'As the Holy Spirit says' (Hebrews 3:7). It is not just that the Holy Spirit spoke in the past. He speaks afresh through what he spoke. This is what makes the Bible so alive. Again, as Martin Luther put it, 'The Bible is alive, it speaks to me; it has feet, it runs after me; it has hands, it lays hold on me.'

What happens when God speaks? *First, he brings faith to those who are not yet Christians.* Paul says, 'Faith comes from hearing the message, and the message is heard through the word of Christ' (Romans 10:17). It is often as people read the Bible that they come to faith in Jesus Christ. That was certainly my experience.

David Suchet, a leading Shakespearean actor and well-known for his title role in *Poirot*, tells how a few years ago he was lying in his bath in a hotel in America, when he had a sudden and impulsive desire to read the Bible. He managed to find a Gideon Bible and he started to read the New Testament. As he read, he came to put his faith in Jesus Christ. He said:

From somewhere I got this desire to read the Bible again. That's the most important part of my conversion. I started with the Acts of the

Apostles and then moved to Paul's Letters – Romans and Corinthians. And it was only after that I came to the gospels. In the New Testament I suddenly discovered the way that life should be followed.[36]

Secondly, he speaks to Christians. As we read the Bible we experience a transforming relationship with God through Jesus Christ. Paul says, 'We, who with unveiled faces all reflect the Lord's glory, are being transformed into his likeness with ever-increasing glory, which comes from the Lord, who is the Spirit' (2 Corinthians 3:18). As we study the Bible, we come into contact with Jesus Christ. It has always struck me as the most extraordinarily wonderful fact that we can speak to and hear from the person whom we read about in the pages of the New Testament – the same Jesus Christ. He will speak to us (not audibly, on the whole, but in our heart) as we read the Bible. We will hear his message for us. As we spend time with him, our characters will become more like his.

Spending time in his presence, listening to his voice, brings many blessings. He often brings joy and peace, even in the middle of a crisis in our lives (Psalm 23:5). When we are not sure which direction we should be going in, God often guides us through his word (Psalm 119:105). The Book of Proverbs even tells us that God's words bring healing to our bodies (Proverbs 4:22).

The Bible also provides us with a defence against spiritual attack. We only have one detailed example of Jesus facing temptation. Jesus faced intense attack by the devil at the start of his ministry (Matthew 4:1-11). Jesus met every temptation with a verse from the Scriptures. I find it fascinating that every one of his replies came from Deuteronomy 6–8. It seems plausible to infer that Jesus had been studying this portion of Scripture and that it was fresh in his mind.

The word of God has great power. The writer of the Book of Hebrews says, 'The word of God is living and active. Sharper than any double-edged sword, it penetrates even to dividing soul and spirit, joints and marrow; it judges the thoughts and attitudes of the heart' (Hebrews 4:12). It has power to pierce all our defences and get through to our hearts. I remember once reading Philippians 2:4, 'Each of you should look not only to your own interests, but also to the interests of others.' It was like an arrow going straight into me as I realised how selfish I was being. In these and many other ways, God's word speaks to us.

Sometimes God speaks to us in a very specific way. God spoke to me very clearly about my father after he died on 21 January 1981. I had become a Christian seven years earlier and my parents' initial reaction was one of complete horror. Gradually, over the years, they began to see a change in me. My mother became a committed Christian long before she died. My father was a man of few words. Initially, he was very unsure about my involvement in the Christian faith. By degrees, he started to become warmer about it. His death was quite sudden. What I found hardest about his death was that I wasn't sure whether he was a Christian or not.

Exactly ten days after his death, I was reading the Bible. I had asked God to speak to me about my father that day because I was still worrying about him. I happened to be reading Romans and I came across the verse, 'Everyone who calls on the name of the Lord will be saved' (Romans 10:13). I sensed at that moment God was saying to me that this verse was for my father; that he had called on the name of the Lord and been 'saved'. About five minutes later my wife, Pippa, came in and said to me, 'I have been reading a verse in Acts 2:21 and I think this verse is for your father. It says, ". . . and everyone who calls on the name of the Lord will be saved."' It was quite extraordinary because that verse only appears twice in the New Testament and God had spoken to both of us through the same words at the same time in different parts of the Bible.

Three days later, we went to a Bible study in a friend's home and the Bible study was on Romans 10:13, that same passage. So three times during those three days God spoke to me about my father through the same words. Nevertheless, on my way to work I was still thinking about my father and worrying about him. As I came out of the underground, I looked up and there was a huge poster saying, 'Whoever calls upon the name of the Lord will be saved' (Romans 10:13). I remember talking to a friend about it and telling him what had happened and he said, 'Do you think the Lord may be trying to speak to you?'!

As God speaks to us and we learn to hear his voice, our relationship with him grows, and our love for him deepens.

HOW IN PRACTICE DO WE HEAR GOD SPEAK THROUGH THE BIBLE?

Time is our most valuable possession. The pressure on time tends to increase as life goes on and we become busier and busier. There is a saying that 'money is power, but time is life'. If we are going to set aside time to read the Bible, we have to plan ahead. If we don't plan it, we will never do it. Don't be depressed if you only keep to 80 per cent of your plan. Sometimes we oversleep!

It is wise to start with a realistic goal. Don't be over-ambitious. It is better to spend a few minutes every day than to spend an hour-and-a-half the first day and then to give up. If you have never studied the Bible before, you might like to set aside seven minutes every day. I am sure that if you do that regularly you will steadily increase it. The more you hear God's word, the more you will want to hear it.

Mark tells us that Jesus got up early and went off to a *solitary place* to pray (Mark 1:35). It is important to try to find somewhere where we can be on our own. I love to go outside if I am in the country. In London it is harder to find 'a solitary place'. I have a corner of a room where I go to read the Bible and pray. I find that first thing in the morning is the best time – before the children are up and the telephone starts ringing. I take a cup of hot chocolate (to wake me up), the Bible, my diary and a notebook. I use the notebook to write down prayers and also things I think God may be saying to me. I use the diary as an aid to praying about each stage of my day, and also for jotting things down that come to my mind. This prevents them acting as a distracting thought.

Start by asking God to speak to you through the passage you are reading. Then read the passage. If you are a beginner I suggest reading a few verses of one of the Gospels each day. You might find it a help to use Bible reading notes which are available at most Christian bookshops.

As you read ask yourself three questions:

1. What does it say? Read it at least once and, if necessary, compare different translations.

2. What does it mean? What did it mean to the person who first wrote it and those who first read it? (This is where the notes may be helpful.)

3. How does it apply to me, my family, my work, my neighbours, the society around me? (This is the most important stage. It is when we see the relevance to our own lives that Bible reading becomes so exciting and we become conscious that we are hearing God's voice.)

Finally, we must put into practice what we hear from God. Jesus said, 'Therefore everyone who hears these words of mine and puts them into practice is like a wise man who built his house on the rock' (Matthew 7:24). As the nineteenth-century preacher D. L. Moody pointed out, 'The Bible was not given to increase our knowledge. It was given to change lives.'

I want to end by looking again at Psalm 1, with which we began this chapter. The psalmist encourages us to 'delight' in the word of God. If we do so, then he says that certain things will happen in our lives.

First, we shall *produce fruit*. The psalmist says, 'They are like trees planted by streams of water, which yield their fruit in season' (v. 3). This promise is that our life will produce fruit; the fruit of the Spirit (as we have seen in Chapter 4). And it will produce fruit in terms of other people's lives being changed as a result. It is not only for our benefit that we read the Bible, but so that we can be a blessing to other people – to our friends, colleagues, neighbours and the society in which we live. This is fruit that will last into eternity (John 15:16).

Secondly, we shall have the strength to *persevere* in our walk with the Lord. God's promise to those of us whose delight is in the law of the Lord is that we will be like trees whose 'leaves do not wither' (v. 3).

If we stay close to Jesus Christ through his word, we will not dry up or lose our spiritual vitality. It is not enough to have great spiritual experiences, although they are very important and very wonderful. Unless we are deeply rooted in Jesus Christ, in his word and in that relationship with him, we won't be able to withstand the storms of life. If we *are* rooted in that relationship, if we *are* delighting in his word, then when the storms come we shall stand.

Thirdly, the psalmist says that the person who delights in the word of God will *prosper* in 'whatever they do' (v. 3). Our lives may not be ones of material prosperity, but we shall prosper in ways that really matter in life – in our relationship with God, in our relationships with other people and in the transforming of our characters into the likeness of Jesus Christ. These things are far more valuable than material wealth.

I hope that you, with the psalmist and with millions of other Christians, will determine to make the Bible your 'delight'.

7

How Does God Guide Us?

We all have to make decisions in life. We are faced with decisions about relationships, marriage, children, use of time, jobs, homes, money, holidays, possessions, giving and so on. Some of these are very big decisions; some smaller. In many cases, it is of the utmost importance that we make the right decisions – for instance in our choice of a marriage partner. We need God's help.

Guidance springs out of our relationship with God. He promises to guide those who are walking with him. He says: 'I will instruct you and teach you in the way you should go' (Psalm 32:8). Jesus promises to lead and guide his followers: 'He calls his own sheep by name and leads them out . . . His sheep follow him because they know his voice' (John 10:3-4). He longs for us to discover his will (Colossians 1:9; Ephesians 5:17). He is concerned about each of us as individuals. He loves us and wants to speak to us about what we should be doing with our lives – about little things as well as big things.

God has a plan for our lives (Ephesians 2:10). Sometimes people are worried by this. They think, 'I'm not sure that I want God's plan for my life. Will his plans be good?' We need not fear. God loves us and wants the very best for our lives. Paul tells us that

God's will for our lives is 'good, pleasing and perfect' (Romans 12:2). He said to his people through the prophet Jeremiah: '"For I know the plans I have for you," declares the Lord, "plans to prosper you and not to harm you, plans to give you hope and a future"' (Jeremiah 29:11).

He is saying, 'Don't you realise that I have a really good plan for your life? I have prepared something wonderful.' This cry from the Lord's heart came because he saw the mess his people had got themselves into when they didn't follow his plans. All around us we see people whose lives are in a muddle. Often people say to me after they have come to Christ, 'I wish I had become a Christian five or ten years earlier. Look at my life now. It is such a mess.'

If we are to find out about God's plans for us, we need to ask him about them. God warned his people about embarking on plans without consulting him: '"Woe to the obstinate children," declares the Lord, "to those who carry out plans that are not mine . . . who go down to Egypt *without consulting me*"' (Isaiah 30:1-2, italics mine). Of course, Jesus is the supreme example of doing the will of his Father. He was consistently 'led by the Spirit' (Luke 4:1) and only did what he saw his Father doing (John 5:19).

We make mistakes because we fail to consult the Lord. We make some plan and think, 'I want to do that but I am not quite sure whether God wants me to do it. I think I'd better not ask him, just in case it's not his will for me!'

God guides us when we are prepared to do his will rather than insisting that our own way is right. The psalmist says, 'He guides the humble' (Psalm 25:9) and 'confides in those who fear [respect] him' (v. 14). God guides those whose attitude is like Mary's: 'I am the Lord's servant and I am willing to do whatever he wants' (Luke 1:38, The Living Bible). The moment we are prepared to do his will, he begins to reveal his plans for our lives.

There is a verse in the Psalms which I go back to time and time again: 'Commit your way to the Lord; trust in him, and he will act' (Psalm 37:5, RSV). Our part is to commit the decision to the Lord and then to trust him. When we have done that, we can wait expectantly for him to act.

Towards the end of our time at university, one of my friends called Nicky, who had become a Christian about the same time that I did, began to get to know very well a girl who was not a Christian. He felt it was not right to marry her unless she shared his faith in Christ. He did not want to put her under any pressure. So he did what the psalmist said and committed it to the Lord. He said, in effect, 'Lord, if this relationship is not right, I pray that you will stop it. If it is right, then I pray she will become a Christian by the last day of the Spring term.' He did not tell her or anyone else about this date. He put his 'trust in him' and waited for him to act. The final day of the Spring term arrived and they happened to be going to a party together that night. Just before midnight she told him she wanted to go for a drive. So they got into the car and she gave him a whole string of directions off the top of her head, just for fun: 'Three turnings left, three turnings right, drive straight for three miles and stop.' He played along and followed them. They ended up in the American cemetery which has one enormous cross in the centre surrounded by hundreds of little crosses. She was shocked and deeply moved by the symbol of the cross, and also by the fact that God had used her instructions to get her attention. She burst into tears. Moments later, she came to faith in Christ. They have now been happily married for many years and still look back and remember how God's hand was on them at that moment.

Given that we are willing to do what God wants us to do, in what ways should we expect God to speak to us and guide us? There are various ways in which he guides us. Sometimes God speaks through one of the ways set out below; sometimes it is a combination. If it is a major decision he may speak through all of them. They are sometimes called the five 'CSs'.

COMMANDING SCRIPTURE

As we have seen, God's general will for all people in all places in all circumstances is revealed in Scripture. He has told us what he thinks about a whole range of issues. From the Bible we know that certain things are wrong. Therefore, we can be quite sure that God will not guide us to do these things. Sometimes a married person says, 'I have fallen in love with this man/woman. We love each other so much. I feel God is leading me to leave my husband/wife and to start this new relationship.' But God has already made his will clear. He has said, 'You shall not commit adultery' (Exodus 20:14). We can be quite sure that God will not guide us to commit adultery.

Sometimes people feel led to save money by not paying their income tax! But God has made it clear that we are to pay any taxes which are due (Romans 13:7). In these and many other areas God has revealed his general will. We do not need to ask his guidance; he has already given it. If we are not sure, we may need to ask someone who knows the Bible better than we do whether there is anything on that issue. Once we have discovered what the Bible says, we need search no further.

Although God's general will is revealed in the Bible, we cannot always find his particular will for our lives there. As we have seen, the Bible tells us that it is his general will for people to get married. Although singleness is a high calling, it is the exception rather than the rule (eg, 1 Corinthians 7:2). We know that Christians are only free to marry other Christians (2 Corinthians 6:14). But the Bible does not tell us whom we should marry!

As we saw in the chapter on the Bible, God still speaks today through the Scriptures. He may speak to us as we read. The psalmist says, 'Your statutes . . . are my counsellors' (Psalm 119:24). That is not to say that we find God's will by opening the Bible anywhere at random and seeing what it says. Rather, as we develop the habit of regular, methodical Bible study we begin to find it quite extraordinary how appropriate each day's reading seems to be for our own particular circumstances.

Sometimes a verse seems almost to leap out of the page at us and we sense God speaking through it. This was certainly my experience, for example, when I sensed God calling me to change jobs. Each time I felt God speaking to me as I read the Bible, I wrote it down. I noted at least fifteen different occasions when I believe God spoke to me through the Bible about his call to me to leave my work as a lawyer and train for ordination in the Church of England.

COMPELLING SPIRIT

Guidance is very personal. When we become Christians, the Spirit of God comes to live within us. When he does so, he begins to communicate with us. We need to learn to hear his voice. Jesus said that his sheep (his followers) would recognise his voice (John 10:4-5). We recognise a good friend's voice immediately on the telephone. If we do not know the person so well, it may be harder and take more time. The more we get to know Jesus, the easier we will find it to recognise his voice.

We find Paul and his companions, for example, planning to enter Bithynia, 'but the Spirit of Jesus would not allow them to' (Acts 16:7). So they went a different way. We do not know how exactly the Spirit spoke to them, but it may have been in one of a number of ways.

Here are three examples of the way in which God speaks by his Spirit.

1. Often he speaks to us as we pray

Prayer is a two-way conversation. Suppose I go to the doctor and say, 'Doctor, I have a number of problems: I have a problem of fungus growing under my toenails, I have piles, my eyes itch, I need a flu jab; I have very bad backaches and I have tennis elbow.' Then, having got through my list of complaints, I look at my watch and say, 'Goodness me, time is getting on. Well, I must be off. Thanks very much for listening.' The doctor might want to say, 'Hang on a second. Why don't you listen to me?' If whenever we pray we only speak to God and never take time to listen, we make the same mistake. In the Bible we find God speaking to his people. For example, on one occasion as the Christians were worshipping the Lord and fasting, the Holy Spirit said, '"Set apart for me Barnabas and Saul for the work to which I have called them." So after they had fasted and prayed, they placed their hands on them and sent them off' (Acts 13:2-3).

Again, we don't know exactly how the Holy Spirit spoke. It may be that as they were praying the thought came into their minds. That is a common way in which God speaks. People sometimes describe it as 'impressions' or feeling it 'in their bones'. It is possible for the Holy Spirit to speak in all these ways.

Obviously such thoughts and feelings need to be tested (1 John 4:1). Is the impression in line with the Bible? Does it promote love? If it does not, it cannot come from a God who is love (1 John 4:16). Is it strengthening, encouraging and comforting (1 Corinthians 14:3)? When we have made the decision, do we know God's peace (Colossians 3:15)?

2. God sometimes speaks to us by giving us a strong desire to do something

'God . . . works in you to *will* and to act according to his good purpose' (Philippians 2:13, italics mine). As we surrender our wills to God, he works in us and often changes our desires. Again, speaking from my own experience, before I became a Christian the last thing in the world I would have wanted to be was an ordained clergyman in the Church of England. Yet when I came to Christ and said I was willing to do what he wanted, I found my desires changed. Now I cannot imagine a greater privilege or a more fulfilling job for me than the one I am doing at the moment.

Sometimes people try to imagine the thing that they would least like to do and then assume that God will ask them to do exactly that. I do not believe God is like that. So don't be frightened and say, 'If I become a Christian, God will make me be a missionary.' If that is what he wants you to do, and your will is surrendered, he will give you a strong desire to do that.

3. God sometimes guides in more unusual ways

There are many examples in the Bible of God guiding individuals in dramatic ways. He spoke to Samuel as a small boy in a way in which he could hear with his physical ears (1 Samuel 3:4-14). He guided Abraham (Genesis 18), Joseph (Matthew 2:19) and Peter (Acts 12:7) through angels. He often spoke through prophets both in the Old Testament and in the New Testament (eg, Agabus – Acts 11:27-28; 21:10-11). He guided through visions (sometimes referred to today as 'pictures'). For example, one night God spoke to Paul in a vision. He saw a man in Macedonia standing and begging him, 'Come over to Macedonia and help us.' Not surprisingly, Paul and his companions took this as guidance that God had called them to preach the gospel in Macedonia (Acts 16:10).

We also find examples of God guiding through dreams (eg, Matthew 1:20; 2:12-13, 22). I was praying for a couple who were good friends of ours. The husband had recently come to faith in Christ. The wife was highly intelligent, but strongly against what had happened to her husband. She became a little hostile towards us. One night I had a dream in which I saw her face quite changed, her eyes full of the joy of the Lord. This encouraged us to continue praying and keeping close to them. A few months later she came to faith in Christ. I remember looking at her and seeing the face I had seen in the dream a few months earlier.

All these are ways in which God guided people in the past and he still does today.

COMMON SENSE

When we become Christians we are not called to abandon common sense. The psalmist warns: 'Do not be like the horse or mule, which have no understanding but must be controlled by bit and bridle or they will not come to you' (Psalm 32:9).

The New Testament writers often encourage us to think and never discourage us from using our minds (eg, 2 Timothy 2:7).

If we abandon common sense, then we get ourselves into absurd situations. In his book *Knowing God*, J. I. Packer quotes an example of a woman who each morning, having consecrated the day to the Lord as soon as she woke, 'would then ask him whether she was to get up or not', and would not stir till 'the voice' told her to dress.

As she put on each article she asked the Lord whether she was to put it on and very often the Lord would tell her to put on the right shoe and leave off the other; sometimes she was to put on both stockings and no shoes; and sometimes both shoes and no stockings. It was the same with all the articles of dress . . .[37]

It is true to say that God's promises of guidance were not given so that we could avoid the strain of thinking. Indeed, John Wesley, the father of Methodism, said that God *usually* guided him by presenting reasons to his mind for acting in a certain way. This is important in every area – especially in the areas of marriage and jobs.

Common sense is one of the factors to be taken into account in the whole area of choosing a partner for life. It is common sense to look at at least three very important areas.

First, *are we spiritually compatible?* Paul warns of the danger of marrying someone who is not a Christian (2 Corinthians 6:14). In practice, if one of the parties is not a Christian, it nearly always leads to a great tension in the marriage. The Christian feels torn between the desire to serve his or her partner and the desire to serve the Lord. But spiritual compatibility means more than the fact that both are Christians. It means that each party respects the other's spirituality, rather than simply being able to say, 'At least they pass the test of being a Christian.'

Secondly, *are we personally compatible?* Obviously, our marriage partner should be a very good friend and someone with whom we have a great deal in common. One of the many advantages of not sleeping together before getting married is that it is easier to concentrate on this area and discover whether or not there is personal compatibility. Often the sexual side can dominate the early stages of a relationship. If the foundations have not been built on friendship then when the initial sexual excitement wears off it can leave the relationship with a very fragile basis.

Thirdly, *are we physically compatible?* By this I mean that we should be attracted to each other. It is not enough to be spiritually and emotionally compatible; the chemistry must work as well. Often the secular world puts it first, but this comes last in the order of priorities. The world often says that it is necessary to sleep together in order to see whether there is sexual compatibility. This is quite wrong. In the biological sense, any incompatibility that can be tested by sexual intercourse is so rare that it can be discounted.

Again, common sense is vital when considering God's guidance about our jobs and careers. The general rule is that we should stay in our current job (if we are in employment) until God calls us to do something else (1 Corinthians 7:17-24). Having said that, in seeking God's will for one's career, it is common sense to take a long-term view of life. It is wise to look ahead ten, fifteen, twenty years and ask the questions: 'Where is my present job taking me? Is that where I want to go in the long term? Or is my long-term vision for something quite different? In which case, where should I be now in order to get there?'

COUNSEL OF THE SAINTS[38]

The Book of Proverbs is full of injunctions to seek wise advice. The writer asserts that 'the wise listen to advice' (Proverbs 12:15). He warns that 'plans fail for lack of counsel', but on the other hand, 'with many advisers they succeed' (Proverbs 15:22). Therefore, he urges, 'Make plans by seeking advice' (Proverbs 20:18).

While seeking advice is very important, we need to remember that ultimately our decisions are between us and God. They are our responsibility. We cannot shift that responsibility onto others or seek to blame them if things go wrong. The 'counsel of the saints' (ie other Christians) is part of guidance – but it is not the only part. Sometimes it may be right to go ahead in spite of the advice of others.

If we are faced with a decision where we need advice, whom should we consult? To the writer of Proverbs, 'fear of the Lord is the beginning of wisdom'. Presumably, therefore, he is thinking of advice from those who 'fear the Lord'. The best advisors are usually godly Christian people with wisdom and experience whom we respect. (It is also wise to seek the advice of parents whom we are to honour, even if we are past the age of being under their authority. Even if they are not Christians, they know us very well and can often have important insights into situations.)

I have found it a real help throughout my Christian life to have someone who is a mature Christian whom I respect and to whom I can go for advice on a whole range of issues. At different times this has been different people. I am so grateful to God for their wisdom and help in many areas. Often God's insight has come as we talked through the issues together.

When it comes to bigger decisions I have found it helpful to seek a range of advice. Over the question of ordination I sought the advice of two such men and my two closest friends, my vicar and those who were involved in the official process of selection.

The people whom we ask for advice should not be chosen on the basis that they will agree with what we have already planned to do! Sometimes one sees a person consulting countless people in the hope that they will eventually find somebody who will endorse their plans. Such advice has little weight and simply enables the person to say, 'And I consulted x and he or she agreed.'

We should consult people on the basis of their spiritual authority or their relationship to us, regardless of what we may anticipate their views to be. When my friends, Nicky and Sila Lee, who now run a church in central London, became Christians, they wondered whether it was right to continue their relationship, because although they were very much in love they were still so young and had no immediate prospects of marriage.

There was a very wise Christian man for whom Nicky had great respect. Nicky knew he had firm views on the subject of relationships and knew he felt it was unwise to be too deeply involved in a relationship while still at university. Nevertheless, Nicky decided to consult him.

The man asked Nicky, 'Have you committed your relationship with Sila to the Lord?' Nicky replied with some hesitation and great honesty, 'I think I have, but sometimes I am not sure,' to which this wise man replied, 'I can see that you love her. I think you should continue in your relationship with her.' Because this advice came from a surprising source it carried additional weight. The advice was very good and they have now had many years of happy married life to prove it.

CIRCUMSTANTIAL SIGNS

God is in ultimate control of all events. The writer of Proverbs points out: 'In your heart you may plan your course, but the Lord determines your steps' (Proverbs 16:9). Sometimes God opens doors (1 Corinthians 16:9) and sometimes he closes them (Acts 16:7). There have been two occasions in my life when God has closed the door on something which I very much wanted, and which I believed at the time was God's will. I tried to force the doors open. I prayed and I struggled and I fought, but they would not open. On both occasions I was bitterly disappointed. But I understand now, years later, why he closed those doors. Indeed I am grateful that he did. However, I am not sure we will ever know this side of heaven why God has closed certain doors in our lives.

Sometimes he opens doors in a remarkable way. The circumstances and the timing point clearly to the hand of God (eg, Genesis 24). Michael Bourdeaux is head of Keston College, a research unit devoted to helping believers in what were communist lands. His work and research are respected by governments all over the world. He studied Russian at Oxford and his Russian teacher, Dr Zernov, sent him a letter which he had received because he thought it would interest him. It detailed how monks were being beaten up by the KGB and subjected to inhuman medical examinations; how they were being rounded up in lorries and dumped many hundreds of miles away. The letter was written very simply, with no adornment, and as he read it Michael Bourdeaux felt he was hearing the true voice of the persecuted church. The letter was signed Varavva and Pronina.

In August 1964, he went on a trip to Moscow, and on his first evening there met up with old friends who explained that the persecutions were getting worse; in particular the old church of St Peter and St Paul had been demolished. They suggested that he go and see it for himself.

So he took a taxi, arriving at dusk. When he came to the square where he had remembered a very beautiful church, he found nothing except a twelve-foot-high fence which hid the rubble where the church had been. Over on the other side of the square, climbing the fence to try to see what was inside, were two women. He watched them, and when they finally left the square he followed them for a hundred yards and eventually caught them up. They asked, 'Who are you?' He replied, 'I am a foreigner. I have come to find out what is happening here in the Soviet Union.'

They took him back to the house of another woman who asked him why he had come. Whereupon he said he had received a letter from the Ukraine via Paris. When she asked who it was from, he replied, 'Varavva and Pronina.' There was silence. He wondered if he had said something wrong. There followed a flood of uncontrolled sobbing. The woman pointed and said, 'This is Varavva, and this is Pronina.'

The population of Russia is over 140 million. The Ukraine, from where the letter was written, is 1,300 kilometres from Moscow. Michael Bourdeaux had flown from England six months after the letter had been written. They would not have met had either party arrived at the demolished church an hour earlier or an hour later. That was one of the ways God called Michael Bourdeaux to set up his life's work.[39]

Don't be in a hurry
Sometimes God's guidance seems to come immediately it is asked for (eg, Genesis 24), but often it takes much longer: sometimes months or even years. We may have a sense that God is going to do something in our lives, but have to wait a long time for it to happen. On these occasions we need patience like that of Abraham who 'after waiting patiently . . . received what was promised' (Hebrews 6:15). While waiting, he was tempted at one point to try to fulfil God's promises by his own means – with disastrous results (see Genesis 16 and 21).

Sometimes we hear God correctly, but we get the timing wrong. God spoke to Joseph in a dream about what would happen to him and his family. He probably expected immediate fulfilment, but he had to wait years. Indeed, while he was in prison it must have been hard for him to believe that his dreams would ever be fulfilled. But thirteen years after the original dream, he saw God's fulfilment. The waiting was part of the preparation (see Genesis 37–50).

In this area of guidance, we all make mistakes. Sometimes, like Abraham, we try to fulfil God's plans by our own wrong methods. Like Joseph we get the timing wrong. Sometimes we feel that we have made too much of a mess of our lives by the time we come to Christ for God to do anything with us. But God is greater than that. He is able to 'restore to you the years which the swarming locust has eaten' (Joel 2:25, RSV). He is able to make something good out of whatever is left of our lives – whether it is a short time or a long time – if we will offer what we have to him and co-operate with his Spirit.

Lord Radstock was staying in a hotel in Norway in the mid-nineteenth century. He heard a little girl playing the piano down in the hallway. She was making a terrible noise: 'Plink . . . plonk . . . plink. . . .' It was driving him mad! A man came and sat beside her and began playing alongside her, filling in the gaps. The result was the most beautiful music. He later discovered that the man playing alongside was the girl's father, Alexander Borodin, composer of the opera *Prince Igor*.

Paul writes that 'in all things God works for the good of those who love him, who have been called according to his purpose' (Romans 8:28). As we falteringly play our part – seeking his will for our lives by reading (commanding Scripture), listening (controlling Spirit), thinking (common sense), talking (counsel of the saints), watching (circumstantial signs) and waiting – God comes and sits alongside us 'and in all things . . . works for the good'. He takes our 'plink . . . plonk . . . plonk . . .' and makes something beautiful out of our lives.

8

Who Is the Holy Spirit?

I had a group of friends at university, five of whom were called Nicky! We used to meet for lunch most days. In February 1974 most of us came to faith in Jesus Christ. We immediately became very enthusiastic about our new-found faith. One of the Nickys, however, was slow to get going. He didn't seem excited about his relationship with God, with reading the Bible or with praying.

One day, someone prayed for him to be filled with the Spirit. He was; and it transformed his life. A great big smile came across his face. He became well-known for his radiance – he still is years later. Thereafter, if there was a Bible study or a prayer meeting or a church in reach, Nicky was there. He loved to be with other Christians. He became the most magnetic personality. People were drawn to him and he helped many others to believe and to be filled with the Spirit in the way that he had been.

What was it that made such a difference to Nicky? I think that he would answer that it was the experience of the Holy Spirit. Many people know a certain amount about God the Father and Jesus the Son. But there is a great deal of ignorance about the Holy Spirit. Hence, three chapters of this book are devoted to the third person of the Trinity.

Some old translations speak of the 'Holy Ghost' and this can make him seem a little frightening. The Holy Spirit is not a ghost but a Person. He has all the characteristics of personhood. He thinks (Acts 15:28), speaks (Acts 1:16), leads (Romans 8:14) and can be grieved (Ephesians 4:30). He is sometimes described as the Spirit of Christ (Romans 8:9) or the Spirit of Jesus (Acts 16:7). He is the way in which Jesus is present with his people. The schoolchild's definition is 'Jesus' other self'.

What is he like? He is sometimes described in the original Greek as the *parakletos* (John 14:16). This is a difficult word to translate. It means 'one called alongside' – a counsellor, a comforter and an encourager. Jesus said the Father will give you 'another' counsellor. The word for 'another' means 'of the same kind'. In other words, the Holy Spirit is just like Jesus.

In this chapter I want to look at the person of the Holy Spirit: who he is and what we can learn about him as we trace his activity through the Bible from Genesis 1 right through to the Day of Pentecost. Because the Pentecostal movement began at the beginning of this century it might be tempting to think that the Holy Spirit is a twentieth-century phenomenon. This is, of course, far from the truth.

HE WAS INVOLVED IN CREATION

We see evidence of the activity of the Holy Spirit in the opening verses of the Bible: 'In the beginning God created the heavens and the earth. Now the earth was formless and empty, darkness was over the surface of the deep, and the Spirit of God was hovering over the waters' (Genesis 1:1-2).

We see in the account of the creation how the Spirit of God caused new things to come into being and brought order out of chaos. He is the same Spirit today. He often brings new things into people's lives and into churches. He brings order and peace into chaotic lives, freeing people from harmful habits and addictions and from the confusion and mess of broken relationships.

When God created humankind, he 'formed a man from the dust of the ground and breathed into his nostrils the breath of life, and the man became a living being' (Genesis 2:7). The Hebrew word implied here for breath is *ruach*, which is also the word for 'Spirit'. The *ruach* of God brings physical life to humanity formed from dust. Likewise, he brings spiritual life to people and churches, both of which can be as dry as dust!

Some years ago I was speaking to a clergyman who was telling me that his life and his church had been like that – a bit dusty. One day he and his wife were filled with the Spirit of God, they found a new enthusiasm for the Bible and their lives were transformed. His church became a centre of life. The youth group, started by his son who had also been filled with the Spirit, experienced explosive growth and became one of the largest in the area.

Many are hungry for life and are attracted to people and churches where they see the life of the Spirit of God.

HE CAME UPON PARTICULAR PEOPLE AT PARTICULAR TIMES FOR PARTICULAR TASKS

When the Spirit of God comes upon people something happens. He does not just bring a nice warm feeling! He comes for a purpose and we see examples of this in the Old Testament.

He filled people for artistic work. The Spirit of God filled Bezalel 'with skill, ability and knowledge in all kinds of crafts – to make artistic designs for work in gold, silver and bronze, to cut and set stones, to work in wood, and to engage in all kinds of craftsmanship' (Exodus 31:3-5).

It is possible to be a talented musician, writer or artist without being filled with the Spirit. But when the Spirit of God fills people for these tasks their work often takes on a new dimension. It has a different effect on others. It has a far greater spiritual impact. This can be true even where the natural ability of the musician or artist is not particularly outstanding. Hearts can be touched and lives changed. No doubt something like this happened through Bezalel.

He also filled individuals for the task of leadership. During the time of the Judges, the people of Israel were often overrun by various foreign nations. At one time it was the Midianites. God called Gideon to lead Israel. Gideon was very conscious of his own weakness and asked, 'How can I save Israel? My clan is the weakest in Manasseh, and I am the least in my family' (Judges 6:15). Yet when the Spirit of God came upon Gideon (v. 34), he became one of the remarkable leaders of the Old Testament.

In leadership, God often uses those who feel weak, inadequate and ill-equipped. When they are filled with the Spirit, they become outstanding leaders in the church. A notable example of this was the Revd E. J. H. 'Bash' Nash. As a nineteen-year-old clerk in an insurance office he had come to faith in Christ and was a man who was full of the Spirit of God. It has been written about him that 'there was nothing particularly impressive about him . . . He was neither athletic nor adventurous. He claimed no academic prowess or artistic talent.'[40] Yet John Stott (whom he led to Christ) said of him: 'Nondescript in outward appearance, his heart was ablaze with Christ.' The obituary in the national and the church press summed up his life like this:

> Bash . . . was a quiet, unassuming clergyman who never made the limelight, hit the headlines or wanted preferment, and yet whose influence within the Church of England during the last 50 years was probably greater than almost any of his contemporaries, for there must be hundreds of men today, many in positions of responsibility, who thank God for him for it was through his ministry that they were led to a Christian commitment.
>
> Those who knew him well, and those who worked with him, never expect to see his like again; for rarely can anyone have meant so much to so many as this quietly spoken, modest and deeply spiritual man.[41]

Elsewhere we see the Holy Spirit filling people with strength and power. The story of Samson is well-known. On one occasion, the Philistines tied him up by binding him with ropes. Then, 'The Holy Spirit of the Lord came upon him in power. The ropes on his arms became like charred flax, and the bindings dropped from his hands' (Judges 15:14).

What is true in the Old Testament physically is often true in the New Testament spiritually. It is not that we are physically bound by ropes, but that we are tied down by fears, habits or addictions which take a grip on our lives. We are controlled by bad temper or by patterns of thought such as envy, jealousy or lust. We know that we are bound when we cannot stop something, even when we want to. When the Spirit of God came upon Samson, the ropes became like charred flax and he was free. The Spirit of God is able to set people free today from anything that binds them.

Later on we see how the Spirit of God came upon the prophet Isaiah to enable him 'to preach good news to the poor . . . to bind up the broken-hearted, to proclaim freedom for the captives and release for the prisoners' and 'to comfort all who mourn' (Isaiah 61:1-3).

We sometimes feel a sense of helplessness when confronted with the problems of the world. I often felt this before I was a Christian. I knew I had little or nothing to offer those whose lives were in a mess. I still feel like that sometimes. But I know that with the help of the Spirit of God, we do indeed have something to give. The Spirit of God enables us to bring the good news of Jesus Christ to bind up those with broken hearts; to proclaim freedom to those who are in captivity to things in their lives which deep down they hate; to release those who are imprisoned by their own wrong-doing; and to bring the comfort of the Holy Spirit (who is after all the comforter) to those who are sad, grieving or mourning. If we are going to help people in a way which lasts eternally, we cannot do so without the Spirit of God.

HE WAS PROMISED BY THE FATHER

We have seen examples of the work of the Spirit of God in the Old Testament. But his activity was limited to particular people at particular times for particular tasks. As we go through the Old Testament we find that God promises that he is going to do something new. The New Testament calls this 'the promise of the Father'. There is an increasing sense of anticipation. *What was going to happen?*

In the Old Testament God made a covenant with his people. He said that he would be their God and that they would be his people. He required that they should keep his laws. Sadly, the people found that they were unable to keep his commands. The Old Covenant was consistently broken.

God promised that one day he would make a *new* covenant with his people. This covenant would be different from the first covenant: 'I will put my law in their minds and write it on their hearts' (Jeremiah 31:33). In other words, under the New Covenant the law would be internal rather than external. If you go on a long hike, you start off by carrying your provisions on your back. They weigh you down and slow you up. But when you have eaten them, not only has the weight gone but you also have a new energy coming from inside. What God promised through Jeremiah was a time when the law would no longer be a weight on the outside but would become a source of energy from inside. *How was this going to happen?*

Ezekiel gives us the answer. He was a prophet, and God spoke through him, elaborating on the earlier promise. 'I will give you a new heart and put a new spirit in you,' he said. 'I will remove from you your heart of stone and give you a heart of flesh. And I will put my Spirit in you and move you to follow my decrees and be careful to keep my laws' (Ezekiel 36:26-27).

God was saying through the prophet Ezekiel that this is what will happen when God puts his Spirit within us. This is how he will change our hearts and make them soft ('hearts of flesh') rather than hard ('hearts of stone'). The Spirit of God will move us to follow his decrees and keep his laws.

Jackie Pullinger has spent the last thirty years working in what was the lawless walled city of Kowloon in Hong Kong. She has given her life to working with prostitutes, heroin addicts and gang members. She began a memorable talk by saying, 'God wants us to have soft hearts and hard feet. The trouble with many of us is that we have hard hearts and soft feet.' Christians should have hard feet in that we should be tough rather than morally weak or 'wet'. Jackie is a glowing example of this in her willingness to go without sleep, food and comfort in order to serve others. Yet she also has a soft heart: a heart filled with compassion. The toughness is in her feet, not her heart.

We have seen what 'the promise of the Father' involves and how it is going to happen. The prophet Joel tells us *to whom it is going to happen*. God says through Joel:

> I will pour out my Spirit on all people.
> Your sons and daughters will prophesy,
> your old men will dream dreams,
> your young men will see visions.
> Even on my servants, both men and women,
> I will pour out my Spirit in those days.
>
> (Joel 2:28-29)

Joel is foretelling that the promise will no longer be reserved for particular people at particular times for particular tasks, but it will be for all. God will pour out his Spirit regardless of sex ('sons and daughters . . . men and women'); regardless of age ('old men . . . young men'); regardless of background, race, colour or rank ('even on my servants'). There will be a new ability to hear God ('prophesy . . . dream . . . see visions'). Joel prophesied that the Spirit would be poured out with great generosity on all God's people.

Yet all these promises remained unfulfilled for at least 300 years. The people waited and waited for the 'promise of the Father' to be fulfilled until at the coming of Jesus there was a burst of activity of the Spirit of God.

With the birth of Jesus, the trumpet sounds. Almost everyone connected with the birth of Jesus was filled with the Spirit of God. John the Baptist, who was to prepare the way, was filled with the

Spirit even before his birth (Luke 1:15). Mary, his mother, was promised: 'The Holy Spirit will come upon you, and the power of the Most High will overshadow you' (Luke 1:35). When Elizabeth her cousin came into the presence of Jesus, who was still in his mother's womb, she too was 'filled with the Holy Spirit' (v. 41) and even John the Baptist's father Zechariah was 'filled with the Holy Spirit' (v. 67). In almost every case there is an outburst of praise or prophecy.

JOHN THE BAPTIST LINKS HIM WITH JESUS

When John was asked whether he was the Christ he replied: 'I baptise you with water. But one more powerful than I will come, the thongs of whose sandals I am not worthy to untie. He will baptise you with the Holy Spirit and with fire' (Luke 3:16). Baptism with water is very important, but it is not enough. Jesus is the Spirit baptiser. The Greek word means 'to overwhelm', 'to immerse' or 'to plunge'. This is what should happen when we are baptised in the Spirit. We should be completely overwhelmed by, immersed in and plunged into the Spirit of God.

Sometimes this experience is like a hard, dry sponge being dropped into water. There can be a hardness in our lives which stops us absorbing the Spirit of God. It may take a little time for the initial hardness to wear off and for the sponge to be filled. So it is one thing for the sponge to be in the water ('baptised'), but it is another for the water to be in the sponge ('filled'). When the sponge is filled with water, the water literally pours out of it.

Jesus was a man completely filled with the Spirit of God. The Spirit of God descended on him in bodily form at his baptism (Luke 3:22). He returned to the Jordan 'full of the Holy Spirit' and was 'led by the Spirit in the desert' (Luke 4:1). He returned to Galilee 'in the power of the Spirit' (v. 14). In a synagogue in Nazareth he read the lesson from Isaiah 61:1, 'The Spirit of the Lord is on me . . .' and said, 'Today this scripture is fulfilled in your hearing' (v. 21).

JESUS PREDICTED HIS PRESENCE

On one occasion Jesus went to a Jewish feast called the Feast of Tabernacles. Thousands of Jews would go to Jerusalem to celebrate the feast, looking back to the time when Moses brought water from a rock. They thanked God for providing water in the past year and prayed that he would do the same in the coming year. They looked forward to a time when water would pour out of the temple (as prophesied by Ezekiel), becoming deeper and deeper and bringing life, fruitfulness and healing wherever it went (Ezekiel 47).

This passage was read at the Feast of Tabernacles and enacted visually. The High Priest would go down to the pool of Siloam and fill a golden pitcher with water. He would then lead the people to the temple where he would pour water through a funnel in the west side of the altar, and into the ground, in anticipation of the great river that would flow from the temple. According to Rabbinic tradition, Jerusalem was the navel of the earth and the temple of Mount Zion was the centre of the navel (its 'belly' or 'innermost being').

On the last day of the feast . . . Jesus stood up and proclaimed, 'If anyone thirst, let him come to me and drink. He who believes in me, as the scripture has said, "Out of his heart [the original word means 'belly' or 'innermost being'] shall flow rivers of living water"' (John 7:38, RSV). He was saying that the promises of Ezekiel and others would not be fulfilled in a place, but in a Person. It is out of the innermost being of Jesus that the river of life will flow. Also, in a derivative sense, the streams of living water will flow from every Christian! ('Whoever believes in me', v. 38). From us, Jesus says, this river will flow, bringing life, fruitfulness and healing to others promised by God through Ezekiel.

John went on to explain that Jesus was speaking about the Holy Spirit 'whom those who believed in him were later to receive' (v. 39). He added that 'up to that time the Spirit had not been given' (v. 39). The promise of the Father had still not been fulfilled. Even after the crucifixion and resurrection of Jesus, the Spirit was not poured out. Later, Jesus told his disciples, 'I am going to send you what my Father has promised; but stay in the city until you have been clothed with power from on high' (Luke 24:49).

Just before he ascended to heaven Jesus again promised, 'You will receive power when the Holy Spirit comes on you' (Acts 1:8). But still they had to wait and pray for another ten days. Then at last on the Day of Pentecost: 'Suddenly a sound like the blowing of a violent wind came from heaven and filled the whole house where they were sitting. They saw what seemed to be tongues of fire that separated and came to rest on each of them. All of them were filled with the Holy Spirit and began to speak in other tongues as the Spirit enabled them' (Acts 2:2-4).

It had happened. The promise of the Father had been fulfilled. The crowd was amazed and mystified.

Peter stood up and explained what had occurred. He looked back to the promises of God in the Old Testament and explained how all their hopes and aspirations were now being fulfilled before their eyes. He explained that Jesus had 'received from the Father the promised Holy Spirit' and had 'poured out what you now see and hear' (Acts 2:33).

When the crowd asked what they needed to do, Peter told them to repent and be baptised in the name of Jesus so that they could receive forgiveness. Then he promised that they would receive the gift of the Holy Spirit. For, he said: 'The promise is for you and your children and for *all* who are far off – for all whom the Lord our God will call' (v. 39, italics mine).

We now live in the age of the Spirit. The promise of the Father has been fulfilled. Every single Christian receives the promise of the Father. It is no longer just for particular people, at particular times for particular tasks. It is for *all* Christians, including you and me.

9

What Does the Holy Spirit Do?

Jesus answered, 'I tell you the truth, no-one can enter the kingdom of God without being born of water and the Spirit. Flesh gives birth to flesh, but the Spirit gives birth to spirit. You should not be surprised at my saying, "You must be born again." The wind blows wherever it pleases. You hear its sound, but you cannot tell where it comes from or where it is going. So it is with everyone born of the Spirit' (John 3:5-8).

A couple of years ago I was in a church in Brighton. One of the Sunday school teachers was telling us about her Sunday school class the previous week. She had been telling the children about Jesus' teaching on being born again in John 3:5-8. She was trying to explain to the children about the difference between physical birth and spiritual birth. In trying to draw them out on the subject she asked, 'Are you born a Christian?' One little boy replied, 'No, Miss. You are born normal!'

The expression 'born again' has become a cliché. It was popularised in America and has been used even to advertise cars. Actually, Jesus was the first person to use the expression of people who were 'born of the Spirit' (John 3:8).

A new baby is born as a result of a man and a woman coming

together in sexual intercourse. In the spiritual realm, when the Spirit of God and the spirit of a man or woman come together, a new spiritual being is created. There is a new birth, spiritually. This is what Jesus is speaking about when he says, 'You must be born again.'

Jesus was saying that physical birth is not enough. We need to be born again by the Spirit. This is what happens when we become Christians. Every single Christian is born again. We may not be able to put our finger on the exact moment it occurred, but just as we know whether or not we are alive physically, so we should know that we are alive spiritually.

When we are born physically, we are born into a family. When we are born again spiritually, we are born into a Christian family. Much of the work of the Spirit can be seen in terms of a family. He assures us of our relationship with our Father and helps us to develop that relationship. He produces in us a family likeness. He unites us with our brothers and sisters, giving each member of the family different gifts and abilities. And he enables the family to grow in size.

In this chapter we will look at each of these aspects of his work in us as Christians. Until we become Christians the Spirit's work is primarily to convict us of our sin and our need for Jesus Christ, to convince us of the truth and to enable us to put our faith in him (John 16:7-15).

SONS AND DAUGHTERS OF GOD

The moment we come to Christ we receive complete forgiveness. The barrier between us and God has been removed. Paul says, 'There is now no condemnation for those who are in Christ Jesus' (Romans 8:1). Jesus took all our sins – past, present and future. God takes all our sins and buries them in the depths of the sea

(Micah 7:19), and as the Dutch author Corrie Ten Boom used to say, 'He puts up a sign saying "No fishing".'

Not only does he wipe the slate clean, but he also brings us into a relationship with God as sons and daughters. Not all men and women are children of God in this sense, although all of us were created by God. It is only to those who receive Jesus, to those who believe in his name, that he gives the 'right to become children of God' (John 1:12). Sonship in the New Testament (which is used in the generic sense to include sons and daughters) is not a natural status, but a spiritual one. We become sons and daughters of God not by being born, but by being born again by the Spirit.

The Book of Romans has been described as the Himalayas of the New Testament. Chapter 8 is Mount Everest and verses 14-17 could well be described as the peak of Everest.

> Because those who are led by the Spirit of God are children of God. For you did not receive a spirit that makes you a slave again to fear, but you received the Spirit of adoption. And by him we cry, 'Abba, Father.' The Spirit himself testifies with our spirit that we are God's children. Now if we are children, then we are heirs – heirs of God and co-heirs with Christ, if indeed we share in his sufferings in order that we may also share in his glory (Romans 8:14-17).

First of all, there is no higher privilege than to be a child of God. Under Roman law if an adult wanted an heir he could either choose one of his own sons or adopt a son. God has only one begotten Son – Jesus, but he has many adopted sons. There is a fairy story in which a reigning monarch adopts waifs and strays and makes them princes. In Christ, the fairy story has become solid fact. We have been adopted into God's family. There could be no higher honour.

Billy Bray was a drunken and loose-living miner from Cornwall, born in 1794. He was always getting involved in fights and domestic quarrels. At the age of twenty-nine he became a Christian. He went home and told his wife, 'You will never see me drunk again, by the help of the Lord.' She never did. His words, his tones and his looks had magnetic power. He was charged with divine electricity. Crowds of miners would come and hear him preach. Many were converted and there were some remarkable healings. He was always praising God and saying that he had abundant reason to rejoice. He described himself as 'a young prince'. He was the adopted son of God, the King of kings and therefore he was a prince, already possessing royal rights and privileges. His favourite expression was, 'I am the son of a King.'[42]

Once we know our status as adopted sons and daughters of God, we realise that there is no status in the world that even compares with the privilege of being a child of the Creator of the universe.

Secondly, as children we have the closest possible intimacy with God. Paul says that by the Spirit we cry, '*Abba*, Father!' This Aramaic word, *Abba* (that we looked at in Chapter 5), is not found in the Old Testament. The use of this word in addressing God was distinctive of Jesus. It is impossible to translate it, but the nearest equivalent translation is probably 'dear Father' or 'Daddy'. The English word 'Daddy' tends to suggest a Western pally relationship to a parent, whereas in Jesus' day the father was an authority figure, and 'Abba', although a term of great intimacy, is not a juvenile word. It was the term Jesus used in addressing God. Jesus allows us to share in that intimate relationship with God when we receive his Spirit. 'For you did not receive a spirit that makes you a slave again to fear, but you received the Spirit of adoption' (v. 15).

Prince Charles has many titles. He is the Heir Apparent to the Crown, his Royal Highness, the Prince of Wales, Duke of Cornwall, Knight of the Garter, Colonel in Chief of the Royal Regiment of Wales, Duke of Rothesay, Knight of the Thistle, Rear Admiral,

Great Master of the Order of Bath, Earl of Chester, Earl of Carrick, Baron of Renfrew, Lord of the Isles and Great Steward of Scotland. We would address him as 'Your Royal Highness', but I suspect to William and Harry he is 'Daddy'. When we become children of God we have an intimacy with our heavenly King. John Wesley, who had been very religious before his conversion, said about his conversion, 'I exchanged the faith of a servant for the faith of a son.'

Thirdly, the Spirit gives us the deepest possible experience of God. 'The Spirit himself testifies with our spirit that we are God's children' (v. 16). He wants us to know, deep within, that we are children of God. In the same way that I want my children to know and experience my love for them and my relationship with them, so God wants his children to be assured of that love and of that relationship.

One man who only experienced this quite late in his life is the South African Bishop Bill Burnett, who was at one time Archbishop of Capetown. I heard him say, 'When I became a bishop I believed in theology [the truth about God], but not in God. I was a practical atheist. I sought righteousness by doing good.' One day, after he had been a bishop for fifteen years, he went to speak at a confirmation service on the text in Romans, 'God has poured out his love [that is, his love for us] into our hearts by the Holy Spirit, whom he has given us' (Romans 5:5). After he had preached, he came home, poured himself a strong drink and was reading the paper when he felt the Lord saying, 'Go and pray.' He went into his chapel, knelt down in silence and sensed the Lord saying to him, 'I want your body.' He could not quite understand why (he is tall and thin and says, 'I'm not exactly Mr Universe'). However, he gave every part of himself to the Lord. 'Then,' he said, 'what I preached about happened. I experienced electric shocks of love.' He found himself flat on the floor and heard the Lord saying,

'You are my son.' When he got up, he knew indeed that something had happened. It proved a turning point in his life and ministry. Since then, through his ministry, many others have come to experience sonship through the witness of the Spirit.

Fourthly, Paul tells us that to be a son or daughter of God is the greatest security. For if we are children of God we are also 'heirs of God and co-heirs with Christ' (Romans 8:17). Under Roman law an adopted son would take his father's name and inherit his estate. As children of God we are heirs. The only difference is that we inherit, not on the death of our father, but on our own death. This is why Billy Bray was thrilled to think that 'his heavenly Father had reserved everlasting glory and blessedness' for him. We will enjoy an eternity of love with Jesus.

Paul adds, 'If indeed we share in his sufferings in order that we may also share in his glory' (v. 17). This is not a condition but an observation. Christians identify with Jesus Christ. This may mean some rejection and opposition here and now, but that is nothing compared to our inheritance as children of God.

DEVELOPING THE RELATIONSHIP

Birth is not just the climax of a period of gestation; it is the beginning of a new life and new relationships. Our relationship with our parents grows and deepens over a long period. This happens as we spend time with them; it does not happen overnight.

Our relationship with God, as we have seen in the early chapters, grows and deepens as we spend time with him. The Spirit of God helps us to develop our relationship with God. He brings us into the presence of the Father. 'For through him [Jesus] we both [Jews and Gentiles alike] have access to the Father by one Spirit' (Ephesians 2:18). Through Jesus, by the Spirit, we have access to the presence of God.

Jesus, through his death on the cross, removed the barrier between us and God. That is why we are able to come into God's presence. Often we don't appreciate that when we are praying.

When I was at university I had a room above Barclays Bank in the High Street. We used to have regular lunch parties in this room, and one day we were discussing whether or not the noise we made could be heard in the bank below. In order to find out, we decided to conduct an experiment. A girl called Kay went down into the bank. As it was lunchtime, it was packed with customers. The arrangement was that we would gradually build up the noise. First, one would jump on the floor, then two, three, four and eventually five. Next we would jump off chairs and then off the table. We wanted to see at which point we could be heard downstairs in the bank.

It turned out that the ceiling was rather thinner than we had thought. The first jump could definitely be heard. The second made a loud noise. After about the fifth, which sounded like a thunderstorm, there was total silence in the bank. Everyone had stopped cashing cheques and was looking at the ceiling, wondering what was going on. Kay was right in the middle of the bank and thought, 'What do I do? If I go out it's going to look very odd, but if I stay it is going to get worse!' She stayed. The noise built up and up. Eventually bits of polystyrene started to fall from the ceiling. At that moment, fearing the ceiling would cave in, she rushed up to tell us that we could indeed be heard in the bank!

Since, through Jesus, the barrier has been removed, God hears us when we pray. We have immmediate access to his presence, by the Spirit. We don't need to jump up and down to get his attention!

Not only does the Spirit bring us into the presence of God, he also helps us to pray (Romans 8:26). What matters is not the place in which we pray, the position in which we pray or whether or not we use set forms of prayer; what matters is whether or not we are praying in the Spirit. All prayer should be led by the Spirit. Without his help prayer can easily become lifeless and dull. In the Spirit we are caught up in the Godhead and it becomes the most important activity of our lives.

Another part of developing our relationship with God is understanding what he is saying to us. Again the Spirit of God enables us to do this. Paul says, 'I keep asking that the God of our Lord Jesus Christ, the glorious Father, may give you the Spirit of wisdom and revelation, so that you may know him better. I pray also that the eyes of your heart may be enlightened . . .' (Ephesians 1:17-18). The Spirit of God is a Spirit of wisdom and revelation. He enlightens our eyes so that, for example, we can understand what God is saying through the Bible.

Before I became a Christian I read and heard the Bible endlessly, but I did not understand it. It meant nothing to me. The reason it did not make sense to me was that I did not have the Spirit of God to interpret it. The Spirit of God is the best interpreter of what God has said.

Ultimately we will never understand Christianity without the Holy Spirit enlightening our eyes. We can see enough to make a step of faith, which is not a blind leap of faith; but real understanding often only follows faith. Anselm of Canterbury said, 'I believe in order that I might understand.'[43] Only when we believe and receive the Holy Spirit can we really understand God's revelation.

The Spirit of God helps us to develop our relationship with God and he enables us to sustain that relationship. People are often worried that they will not be able to keep going in the Christian life. They are right to worry. We can't keep going by ourselves, but God by his Spirit keeps us going. It is the Spirit who brings us into a relationship with God and it is the Spirit who maintains that relationship. We are utterly dependent on him.

THE FAMILY LIKENESS

I always find it fascinating to observe how children can look like both parents at the same time when the parents themselves may look so different. Even husbands and wives sometimes grow to look like each other as they spend time together over the years!

As we spend time in the presence of God, the Spirit of God transforms us. As Paul writes, 'And we, who with unveiled faces all reflect the Lord's glory, are being transformed into his likeness with ever-increasing glory, which comes from the Lord, who is the Spirit' (2 Corinthians 3:18). We are transformed into the moral likeness of Jesus Christ. The fruit of the Spirit is developed in our lives. Paul tells us that 'the fruit of the Spirit is love, joy, peace, patience, kindness, goodness, faithfulness, gentleness and self-control' (Galatians 5:22). These are the characteristics that the Spirit of God develops in our lives. It is not that we become perfect immediately, but over a period of time there should be a change.

The first and most important fruit of the Spirit is love. Love lies at the heart of the Christian faith. The Bible is the story of God's love for us. His desire is that we should respond by loving him and loving our neighbour. The evidence of the work of the Spirit in our lives will be an increasing love for God and an increasing love for others. Without this love everything else counts for nothing.

Second in Paul's list is joy. The journalist, Malcolm Muggeridge, wrote: 'The most characteristic and uplifting of the manifestations of conversion is rapture – an inexpressible joy which suffuses our whole being, making our fears dissolve into nothing, and our expectations all move heavenwards.'[44] This joy is not dependent on our outward circumstances; it comes from the Spirit within. Richard Wurmbrand, who was imprisoned for many years and frequently tortured on account of his faith, wrote of this joy: 'Alone in my cell, cold, hungry and in rags, I danced for joy every night

135

. . . sometimes I was so filled with joy that I felt I would burst if I did not give it expression.'[45]

The third fruit listed is peace. Detached from Christ, inner peace is a kind of spiritual marshmallow full of softness and sweetness but without much actual substance. The Greek word and Hebrew equivalent *shalom* means 'wholeness', 'soundness', 'well-being' and 'oneness with God'. There is a longing within every human heart for peace like that. Epictetus, the first-century pagan thinker, said, 'While the Emperor may give peace from war on land and sea, he is unable to give peace from passion, grief and envy. He cannot give peace of heart, for which man yearns more than ever for outward peace.'

It is wonderful to see those whose characters have been transformed into the likeness of Jesus Christ as these and the other fruit of the Spirit have grown in their lives. A woman in her eighties in our congregation said of a former vicar, 'He gets more and more like our Lord.' I cannot think of a higher compliment than that. It is the work of the Spirit of God to make us more and more like Jesus so that we carry the fragrance of the knowledge of him wherever we go (2 Corinthians 2:14).

UNITY IN THE FAMILY

When we come to Christ and become sons and daughters of God we become part of a huge family. God's desire, like that of every normal parent, is that there should be unity in his family. Jesus prayed for unity among his followers (John 17). Paul pleaded with the Ephesian Christians to 'make every effort to keep *the unity of the Spirit* through the bond of peace' (Ephesians 4:3, italics mine).

The same Holy Spirit lives in every Christian wherever they are; whatever the denomination, background, colour or race. The same Spirit is in every child of God and his desire is that we should be united. Indeed, it is a nonsense for the church to be divided because there is '*one* body and *one* Spirit . . . *one* hope . . . *one* Lord, *one* faith, *one* baptism; *one* God and Father of *all*, who is over *all* and through *all* and in *all*' (Ephesians 4:4-6, italics mine).

The same Spirit indwells Christians in Russia, China, Africa, America, the UK or wherever. In one sense it is not so important what denomination we are – Roman Catholic or Protestant; Lutheran, Methodist, Baptist, Pentecostal, Anglican or House Church. What is more important is whether or not we have the Spirit of God. If people have the Spirit of God living within them, they are Christians, and our brothers and sisters. It is a tremendous privilege to be part of this huge family; one of the great joys of coming to Christ is to experience this unity. There is a closeness and depth of relationship in the Christian church which I have never found outside of it. We must make every effort to keep the unity of the Spirit at every level: in our small groups, congregations, local church and the worldwide church.

GIFTS FOR ALL THE CHILDREN

Although there is often a family likeness and, hopefully, unity in the family, there is also great variety. No two children are identical – not even 'identical' twins are exactly alike. So it is in the body of Christ. Every Christian is different; each has a different contribution to make, each has a different gift. In the New Testament there are lists of some of the gifts of the Spirit. In 1 Corinthians Paul lists nine gifts:

> Now to each one the manifestation of the Spirit is given for the common good. To one there is given through the Spirit the message of wisdom, to another the message of knowledge by means of the same Spirit, to another faith by the same Spirit, to another gifts of healing by

that one Spirit, to another miraculous powers, to another prophecy, to another the distinguishing between spirits, to another speaking in different kinds of tongues, and to still another the interpretation of tongues. All these are the work of one and the same Spirit, and he gives them to each one, just as he determines (1 Corinthians 12:7-11).

Elsewhere he mentions other gifts: those given to apostles, teachers, helpers, administrators (1 Corinthians 12:28-30), evangelists and pastors (Ephesians 4), gifts of serving, encouraging, giving, leadership, showing mercy (Romans 12:7), hospitality and speaking (1 Peter 4). No doubt these lists were not intended to be exhaustive.

All good gifts are from God, even if some, such as miracles, more obviously demonstrate the unusual acts of God in his world. Spiritual gifts include natural talents which have been transformed by the Holy Spirit. As the German theologian Jurgen Moltmann points out, 'In principle every human potentiality and capacity can become charismatic [ie, a gift of the Spirit] through a person's call, if only they are used in Christ.'

These gifts are given to all Christians. The expression 'to each one' runs like a thread through 1 Corinthians 12. Every Christian is part of the body of Christ. There are many different parts, but one body (v. 12). We are baptised by (or in) one Spirit (v. 13). We are all given the one Spirit to drink (v. 13). There are no first- and second-class Christians. All Christians receive the Spirit. All Christians have spiritual gifts.

There is an urgent need for the gifts to be exercised. One of the major problems in the church at large is that so few are exercising their gifts. The church growth expert Eddie Gibbs once said, 'The level of unemployment in the nation pales into insignifance in comparison with that which prevails in the church.'[46] As a result, a few people are left doing everything and are totally exhausted, while the rest are under-utilised. The church has been likened to a football match, in which thousands of people desperately in need of exercise watch twenty-two people desperately in need of a rest!

The church cannot operate in maximum effectiveness until each person is playing his or her part. As David Watson, the writer and church leader, pointed out, 'In different traditions, the church for years has been either pulpit-centred or altar-centred. In both situations the dominant role has been played by the minister or priest.'[47] The church will only operate with maximum effectiveness when every person is using his or her gifts.

The Spirit of God gives each of us gifts. God does not require us to have many gifts, but he does require us to use what we have and to desire more (1 Corinthians 12:31; 14:1).

THE GROWING FAMILY

It is natural for families to grow. God said to Adam and Eve, 'Be fruitful and multiply.' It should be natural for the family of God to grow. Again, this is the work of the Spirit. Jesus said, 'You will receive power when the Holy Spirit comes on you; and you will be my witnesses in Jerusalem, and in all Judea and Samaria, and to the ends of the earth' (Acts 1:8).

The Spirit of God gives us both a desire and the ability to tell others. The playwright Murray Watts tells the story of a young man who was convinced of the truth of Christianity, but was paralysed with fear at the very thought of having to admit to being 'a Christian'. The idea of telling anyone about his new-found faith, with all the dangers of being dubbed a religious nutcase, appalled him.

For many weeks he tried to banish the thought of religion from his mind, but it was no use. It was as if he heard a whisper in his conscience, repeating over and over again, 'Follow me.'

At last he could stand it no longer and he went to a very old man, who had been a Christian for the best part of a century. He told him of his nightmare, this terrible burden of 'witnessing to the light', and how it stopped him from becoming a Christian. The man sighed and shook his head. 'This is a matter between you and Christ,' he said. 'Why bring all these other people into it?' The young man nodded slowly.

'Go home,' said the old man. 'Go into your bedroom alone. Forget the world. Forget your family, and make it a secret between you and God.'

The young man felt a weight fall from him as the old man spoke. 'You mean, I don't have to tell anyone?'

'No,' said the old man.

'No one at all?'

'Not if you don't want to.' Never had anyone dared to give him this advice before.

'Are you *sure?*' asked the young man, beginning to tremble with anticipation. 'Can this be right?'

'It is right for you,' said the old man.

So the young man went home, knelt down in prayer and was converted to Christ. Immediately, he ran down the stairs and into the kitchen, where his wife, father and three friends were sitting. 'Do you realise,' he said, breathless with excitement, 'that it's possible to be a Christian without telling anyone?'[48]

When we experience the Spirit of God we want to tell others. As we do, the family grows. The Christian family should never be static. It should be continually growing and drawing in new people, who themselves receive the power of the Holy Spirit and go out and tell others about Jesus.

I have stressed throughout this chapter that every Christian is indwelt by the Holy Spirit. Paul says, 'And if anyone does not have the Spirit of Christ, that person does not belong to Christ'

(Romans 8:9). Yet not every Christian is filled with the Spirit. Paul writes to the Christians at Ephesus and says, 'Be filled with the Spirit' (Ephesians 5:18). In the next chapter we will look at how we can be filled with the Spirit.

We started the previous chapter with Genesis 1:1-2 (the first verses in the Bible) and I want to end this chapter by looking at Revelation 22:17 (one of the last verses in the Bible). The Spirit of God is active throughout the Bible from Genesis to Revelation.

'The Spirit and the bride say, "Come!" And let those who hear say, "Come!" Let those who are thirsty come; and let all who wish take the free gift of the water of life' (Revelation 22:17).

God wants to fill every one of us with his Spirit. Some people are longing for this. Some are not so sure that they want it – in which case they do not really have a thirst. If you do not have a thirst for more of the Spirit's fullness why not pray for such a thirst? God takes us as we are. When we thirst and ask, God will give us 'the free gift of the water of life'.

10

How Can I Be Filled with the Spirit?

The evangelist J. John once addressed a conference on the subject of preaching. One of the points he made was that so often preachers exhort their hearers to do something, but they never tell them *how* to do it. They say, 'Read your Bible.' He wants to ask, 'Yes, but how?' They say, 'Pray more.' He asks, 'Yes, but how?' They say, 'Tell people about Jesus.' He asks, 'Yes, but how?' In this chapter I want to look at the question of *how* we can be filled with the Spirit.[49]

We have an old gas boiler in our house. The pilot light is on all the time. But the boiler is not always giving out heat and power. Some people have only got the pilot light of the Holy Spirit in their lives, whereas when people are filled with the Holy Spirit, they begin to fire on all cylinders (if you will forgive my mixing metaphors!). When you look at them you can almost see and feel the difference.

The Book of Acts has been described as Volume I of the history of the church. In it we see several examples of people experiencing the Holy Spirit. In an ideal world every Christian would be filled with the Holy Spirit from the moment of conversion. Sometimes it happens like that (both in the New Testament and now), but not always – even in the New Testament. We have already looked at the first occasion of the outpouring of the Holy Spirit at Pentecost in Acts 2. As we go through Acts we will see other examples.

When Peter and John prayed for the Samaritan believers and the Holy Spirit came upon them, Simon the Magician was so impressed that he offered money in order to be able to do the same thing (Acts 8:14-18). Peter warned him that it was a terrible thing to try and buy God's gift for money. But the account shows that something very wonderful must have happened.

In the next chapter (Acts 9) we see one of the most remarkable conversions of all times. When Stephen the first Christian martyr was stoned, Saul approved his death (Acts 8:1) and afterwards began to destroy the church. Going from house to house, he dragged men and women off to prison (v. 3). At the beginning of chapter 9 we find him still 'breathing out murderous threats against the Lord's disciples'.

Within the space of a few days, Saul was preaching in synagogues that 'Jesus is the Son of God' (v. 20). He caused total astonishment, with people asking, 'Isn't he the man who caused havoc in Jerusalem among those who call on this name [of Jesus]?'

What had happened in those few days to change him so completely? First, he had encountered Jesus on the road to Damascus. Secondly, he had been filled with the Spirit (v. 17). That moment, 'something like scales fell from Saul's eyes, and he could see again' (v. 18). It sometimes happens that people who were not Christians, or who were even strongly anti-Christian, have a complete turnabout in their lives when they come to Christ and are filled with the Spirit. They can become powerful advocates of the Christian faith.

At Ephesus, Paul came across a group who 'believed', but who had not even heard of the Holy Spirit. He placed his hands on them, the Holy Spirit came on them and they spoke in tongues and prophesied (Acts 19:1-7). There are people today who are in a similar position. They may have 'believed' for some time or even all their lives. They may have been baptised, confirmed and gone to church from time to time or even regularly. Yet they may know little or nothing about the Holy Spirit.

Another incident occurs early in the Book of Acts and I want to look at it in a little more detail. It is the first occasion when Gentiles were filled with the Spirit. God did something extraordinary which started with a vision given to a man called Cornelius (who had been prepared by the first vision). God also spoke to Peter through a vision and told him he wanted him to go and speak to the Gentiles at the house of this man Cornelius. Halfway through Peter's talk something remarkable happened: 'The Holy Spirit came on all who heard the message. The circumcised believers [ie, the Jews] who had come with Peter were astonished that the gift of the Holy Spirit had been poured out even on the Gentiles. For they heard them speaking in tongues and praising God' (Acts 10:44-46). In the rest of the chapter I want to examine three aspects of what happened.

THEY EXPERIENCED THE POWER OF THE HOLY SPIRIT

Peter had to stop his talk because it was obvious that something was happening. The filling of the Spirit rarely happens imperceptibly, although the experience is different for everyone.

In the description of the Day of Pentecost (Acts 2), Luke uses the language of a heavy tropical rainstorm. It is a picture of the power of the Spirit flooding their beings. There were physical manifestations. They heard a gale (v. 2) which was not a real gale, but it resembled one. It was the mighty invisible power of the ruach of God; the same word as we have seen for wind, breath and spirit in the Old Testament. Sometimes, when people are filled, they shake like a leaf in the wind. Others find themselves breathing deeply as if almost physically breathing in the Spirit.

They also saw something that resembled fire (v. 3). Physical heat sometimes accompanies the filling of the Spirit and people experience it in their hands or some other part of their bodies. One person described a feeling of 'glowing all over'. Another said she experienced 'liquid heat'. Still another described 'burning in my arms when I was not hot'. Fire perhaps symbolises the power, passion and purity which the Spirit of God brings to our lives.

For many, the experience of the Spirit may be an overwhelming experience of the love of God. Paul prays for the Christians at Ephesus that they might have 'power, together with all the saints, to grasp how wide and long and high and deep is the love of Christ' (Ephesians 3:18). The love of Christ is wide enough to reach every person in the world. It reaches across every continent to people of every race, colour, tribe and background. It is long enough to last throughout a lifetime and into eternity. It is deep enough to reach us however far we have fallen. It is high enough to lift us into the heavenly places. We see this love supremely in the cross of Christ. We know Christ's love for us because he was willing to die for us. Paul prayed that we would 'grasp' the extent of this love.

Yet he does not stop there. He goes on to pray that we would '*know* this love that *surpasses knowledge*' – that you would 'be filled to the measure of all the fulness of God' (v. 19). It is not enough to understand his love; we need to experience his love that 'surpasses knowledge'. It is often as people are filled with the Spirit – 'filled to the measure of all the fulness of God' (v. 19) that they experience in their heart this transforming love of Christ.

Thomas Goodwin, one of the Puritans of 300 years ago, illustrated this experience. He pictured a man walking along a road hand in hand with his little boy. The little boy knows that this man is his father, and that his father loves him. But suddenly the father stops, picks up the boy, lifts him into his arms, embraces him, kisses him and hugs him. Then he puts him down again, and they continue walking. It is a wonderful thing to be walking along holding your father's hand; but it is an incomparably greater thing to have his arms enfolded around you.

'He has embraced us,' says Spurgeon and he pours his love upon us and he 'hugs' us. Martyn Lloyd-Jones quotes these examples among many others in his book on Romans, and comments on the experience of the Spirit:

> Let us realize then the profound character of the experience. This is not light and superficial and ordinary; it is not something of which you can say, 'Don't worry about your feelings.' Worry about your feelings? You will have such a depth of feeling that for a moment you may well imagine that you have never 'felt' anything in your life before. It is the profoundest experience that a man can ever know.[50]

THEY WERE RELEASED IN PRAISE

When these Gentiles were filled with the Spirit they started 'praising God'. Spontaneous praise is the language of people who are excited and thrilled about their experience of God. It should involve our whole personality, including our emotions. I am asked, 'Is it right to express emotions in church? Isn't there a danger of emotionalism?'

The danger for most of us in our relationship with God is not emotionalism, but a lack of emotion – a lack of feeling. Our relationship with God can be rather cold. Every relationship of love involves our emotions. Of course, there must be more than emotions. There must be friendship, communication, understanding and service. But if I never showed any emotion towards my wife, there would be something lacking in my love for her. If we do not experience any emotion in our relationship with

God, then our whole personality is not involved. We are called to love, praise and worship God with *all* of our beings.

It could be argued that emotions are all right in private, but what about the public demonstration of emotion? After a conference at Brighton attended by the Archbishop of Canterbury there was a correspondence in *The Times* about the place of emotions in church. Under the title 'Carey's charisms' one man wrote:

> Why is it that if a cinema comedy produces laughter, the film is regarded as successful; if a theatre tragedy brings tears to the audience the production is regarded as touching; if a football match thrills the spectators, the game is reviewed as exciting; but if the congregation are moved by the glory of God in worship, the audience are accused of emotionalism?

Of course, there is such a thing as emotionalism, where emotions take precedence over the solid foundation of teaching from the Bible. But as the former Bishop of Coventry Cuthbert Bardsley once said, 'The chief danger of the Anglican church is not delirious emotionalism.' One might add, 'Nor in many other churches.' Our worship of God should involve our whole personality, mind, heart, will and emotions.

THEY RECEIVED A NEW LANGUAGE

As on the Day of Pentecost and with the Ephesian Christians (Acts 19), when the Gentiles were filled with the Spirit they received the gift of tongues. The word for 'tongues' is the same word as that for 'languages' and it means the ability to speak in a language you have never learned. It may be an angelic language (1 Corinthians 13:1) which presumably is not recognisable or it may be a recognisable human language (as at Pentecost). A young woman called Penny, in our congregation, was praying with another girl. She ran out of words in English and started praying in tongues. The girl smiled and then opened her eyes and started laughing. She said, 'You have just spoken to me in Russian.' The girl, although English, spoke fluent Russian and had a great love for the language. Penny asked, 'What have I been saying?' The girl told her that she had been saying, 'My dear child,' over and over again. Penny does not speak a single word of Russian. For that young woman those three words were of great significance. She was assured that she was important to God.

The gift of tongues has brought great blessing to many people. It is, as we have seen, one of the gifts of the Spirit. It is not the only gift or even the most important gift. Not all Christians speak in tongues nor is it necessarily a sign of being filled with the Spirit. It is possible to be filled with the Spirit and not speak in tongues. Nevertheless, for many, both in the New Testament and in Christian experience, it accompanies an experience of the Holy Spirit and may be the first experience of the more obviously supernatural activity of the Spirit. Many today are puzzled by the gift. Hence, I have devoted quite a lot of space in this chapter to the subject. In 1 Corinthians 14 Paul deals with a number of questions which are often raised.

What exactly is speaking in tongues?

It is a form of prayer (one of the many different forms of prayer found in the New Testament), according to Paul, 'for those who speak in a tongue do not speak to people but *to God*' (1 Corinthians 14:2, italics mine). It is a form of prayer which builds up the individual Christian (v. 4). Obviously, the gifts which directly edify the church are even more important, but this does not make tongues unimportant. The benefit of tongues is that it is a form of prayer which transcends the limitation of human language. This seems to be what Paul means when he says 'For if I pray in a tongue, my spirit prays, but my mind is unfruitful' (1 Corinthians 14:14).

Everybody, to a greater or lesser extent, is limited by language. I am told that the average Englishman knows 5,000 English words. Winston Churchill apparently used 50,000 words. But even he was limited to that extent. Often people experience frustration that they cannot express what they really feel, even in a human relationship. They feel things in their spirits, but they do not know how to put them into words. This is often true also in our relationship with God.

This is where the gift of tongues can be a great help. It enables us to express to God what we really feel in our spirits without going through the process of translating it into English. (Hence Paul says, 'My mind is unfruitful.') It is not mindless; it is unfruitful because it is not going through the process of translation into an intelligible language.

In what areas does it help?
There are three areas in which many people have found this gift especially helpful.

First, in the area of *praise and worship*. We are particularly limited in our language. When children (or even adults) write thank-you letters it is not long before they run out of language, and we find that words such as 'lovely', 'wonderful' or 'brilliant' are repeated over and over again. In our praise and worship of God we can often find language limiting.

We long to express our love, worship and praise of God, particularly when we are filled with the Spirit. The gift of tongues enables us to do this without the limitation of human language.

Secondly, it can be a great help when *praying under pressure*. There are times in our lives when it is hard to know exactly how to pray. It can be because we are burdened by many pressures, anxieties or griefs. Not long ago I prayed for a man aged twenty-six whose wife had died of cancer after only one year of married life. He asked for and instantly received the gift of tongues and all the things that he had pushed down in his life seemed to pour out. He told me afterwards what a relief it had been to be able to unburden all those things.

I too have found this in my own experience. In 1987 during a staff meeting at our church, I received a message to say that my mother had had a heart attack and was in hospital. As I dashed up to the main road and caught a taxi to the hospital, I have never been more grateful for the gift of tongues. I desperately wanted to pray, but felt too shocked to form any sentences in English. The gift of tongues enabled me to pray all the way to the hospital and to bring the situation to God in a time of crisis.

Thirdly, many people have found the gift a help in *praying for other people.* It is hard to pray for others – especially if you have not seen them or heard from them for some time. After a while, 'Lord, bless them' might be our most elaborate prayer. It can be a real help to start praying in tongues for them. Often, as we do that, God gives us the words to pray in English.

It is not selfish to want to pray in tongues. Although, 'Those who speak in a tongue edify themselves' (1 Corinthians 14:4), the indirect effects of this can be very great. Jackie Pullinger describes the transformation in her ministry when she began to use the gift:

By the clock I prayed 15 minutes a day in the language of the Spirit and still felt nothing as I asked the Spirit to help me intercede for those he wanted to reach. After about six weeks of this I began to lead people to Jesus without trying. Gangsters fell to their knees sobbing in the streets, women were healed, heroin addicts were miraculously set free. And I knew it all had nothing to do with me.

It was also the gateway for her to receive other gifts of the Spirit:

> With my friends I began to learn about the other gifts of the Spirit and we experienced a remarkable few years of ministry. Scores of gangsters and well-to-do people, students and churchmen, were converted and all received a new language to pray in private and other gifts to use when meeting together. We opened several homes to house heroin addicts and all were delivered from drugs painlessly because of the power of the Holy Spirit.[51]

Does Paul approve of speaking in tongues?

The context of 1 Corinthians 14 is excessive public use in church of the gift of tongues. Paul says, '*In the church* I would rather speak five intelligible words to instruct others than ten thousand words in a tongue' (v. 19, italics mine). There would be little point in Paul arriving at Corinth and giving his sermon in tongues. They would not be able to understand unless there was someone to interpret. So he lays down guidelines for the public use of tongues (v. 27).

Nevertheless, Paul makes it clear that speaking in tongues should not be forbidden (v. 39). With regard to the private use of this gift (on our own with God), he strongly encourages it. He says, 'I would like every one of you to speak in tongues' (v. 5) and, 'I thank God that I speak in tongues more than all of you' (v. 18). This does not mean that every Christian has to speak in tongues or that we are second-class Christians if we do not speak in tongues. There is no such thing as first- and second-class Christians. Nor does it mean that God loves us any less if we don't yet speak in tongues. Nevertheless, the gift of tongues is a blessing from God.

How do we receive the gift of tongues?

Some say, 'I don't want the gift of tongues.' God will never force you to receive a gift. Tongues is just one of the wonderful gifts of the Spirit, and not the only one by any means, as we saw in the last chapter. Like every gift, it has to be received by faith.

Not every Christian speaks in tongues, but there is no reason why anyone who wants this gift should not receive it. Paul is not saying that speaking in tongues is the be-all and end-all of the Christian life; he is saying that it is a very helpful gift. If you would like to receive it, there is no reason why you should not.

Like all the gifts of God, we have to co-operate with his Spirit. God does not force his gifts on us. When I first became a Christian I read somewhere that the gifts of the Spirit went out in the apostolic age (ie, the first century). They were not for today. When I heard about speaking in tongues I decided to confirm that they were not for today, so I prayed for the gift and then kept my mouth firmly shut! I didn't start praying in tongues and felt that this proved that the gifts had gone out with the apostles.

One day two friends of mine, who had just been filled with the Spirit and received the gift of tongues, came round to see me. I told them quite firmly that the gifts of the Spirit had gone out with the apostolic age, but I could see the difference it had made to them. There was a new radiance about them, and there still is years later. I decided to ask the people who had prayed for them to pray for me to be filled with the Spirit and to receive the gift of tongues. As they did, I experienced the power of the Holy Spirit. They explained to me that if I wanted to receive the gift of tongues, I had to co-operate with the Spirit of God and open my mouth and start to speak to God in any language but English or another known to me. As I did, I received the gift of tongues also.

WHAT ARE THE COMMON HINDRANCES TO BEING FILLED WITH THE SPIRIT?

On one occasion Jesus was speaking to his disciples on the subject of prayer and the Holy Spirit (Luke 11:9-13). In that passage he deals with some of the principal difficulties we may have in receiving from God.

Doubt

There are many doubts people have in this whole area, the principal one being, 'If I ask will I receive?'

Jesus says simply: 'I say to you: Ask and it will be given to you.'

Jesus must have seen that they were a little sceptical because he repeats it in a different way: 'Seek and you will find.'

And again he says a third time: 'Knock and the door will be opened to you.'

He knows human nature so he goes on a fourth time: 'For everyone who asks receives.'

They are not convinced so he says it a fifth time: 'He who seeks finds.'

Again a sixth time: 'To him who knocks, the door will be opened.'

Why does he say it six times? Because he knows what we are like. We find it very difficult to believe that God would give us anything – let alone something as unusual and wonderful as his Holy Spirit and the gifts that come with the Spirit.

Fear

Even if we have cleared the first hurdle of doubt, some of us trip up on the next hurdle of fear. The fear is about what we will receive. Will it be something good?

Jesus uses the analogy of a human father. If a child asks for a fish, no father would give him a snake. If a child asks for an egg, no father would give him a scorpion (Luke 11:11-12). It is unthinkable that we would treat our children like that. Jesus goes on to say that in comparison with God we are evil! If we would not treat our children like that, it is inconceivable that God would treat us like that. He is not going to let us down. If we ask for the Holy Spirit and all the wonderful gifts he brings, that is exactly what we will receive (Luke 11:13).

Inadequacy

Of course it is important that there is no unforgiveness or other sin in our lives, and that we have turned our back on all that we know is wrong. However, even after we have done that, we often have a vague feeling of unworthiness and inadequacy. We cannot believe that God would give us anything. We can believe that he would give gifts to very advanced Christians, but not to us. But Jesus does not say, 'How much more will your Father in heaven give the Holy Spirit to all very advanced Christians.' He says, 'How much more will your Father in heaven give the Holy Spirit to *those who ask him*' (Luke 11:13, italics mine).

If you would like to be filled with the Spirit you might like to find someone who would pray for you. If you don't have anyone who would be able to pray for you, there is nothing to stop you from praying on your own. Some are filled with the Spirit without receiving the gift of tongues. The two do not necessarily go together. Yet in the New Testament and in experience they often do go together. There is no reason why we should not pray for both.

If you are praying on your own:

1. Ask God to forgive you for anything that could be a barrier to receiving.

2. Turn from any area of your life that you know is wrong.

3. Ask God to fill you with his Spirit. Go on seeking him until you find. Go on knocking until the door opens. Seek God with all your heart.

4. If you would like to receive the gift of tongues, ask. Then open your mouth and start to praise God in any language but

English or any other language known to you.

5. Believe that what you receive is from God. Don't let anyone tell you that you made it up. (It is most unlikely that you have.)

6. Persevere. Languages take time to develop. Most of us start with a very limited vocabulary. Gradually it develops. Tongues is like that. It takes time to develop the gift. But don't give up.

7. If you have prayed for any other gift, seek opportunities to use it. Remember that all gifts have to be developed by use.

Being filled with the Spirit is not a one-off experience. Peter was filled with the Spirit three times in the space of chapters 2-4 in the Book of Acts (Acts 2:4; 4:8, 31). When Paul says, 'Be filled with the Spirit' (Ephesians 5:18), he uses the present continuous tense, urging them and us to go on and on being filled with the Spirit.

11

How Can I Resist Evil?

There is a close connection between good and God and between evil and the devil. Indeed, in each case the difference is only one letter! Behind the power of good lies Goodness himself. Directly or indirectly behind our own evil desires and the temptations of the world lies evil personified – the devil.

Because there is so much evil in the world some find it easier to believe in the devil than in God. 'As far as God goes, I am a non-believer . . . but when it comes to the devil – well that's something else . . . the devil keeps advertising . . . the devil does lots of commercials,' said William Peter Blatty who wrote and produced *The Exorcist*.[52]

On the other hand, many Westerners find belief in the devil more difficult than belief in God. This may be partly because of a false image of what the devil is like. If the image of God as a white bearded old man sitting on a cloud is absurd and incredible, so also is the image of a horned devil trudging through Dante's inferno. We are not dealing with an alien from outer space but with a real personal force of evil who is active in the world today.

Once we have come to believe in a transcendent God, in some ways it is only logical to accept belief in a devil.

Belief in a great transcendent power of evil adds nothing whatever to the difficulties imposed by belief in a transcendent power of good. Indeed, it eases them somewhat. For if there were no Satan, it would be hard to resist the conclusion that God is a fiend both because of what he does, in nature, and what he allows, in human wickedness.[53]

According to the biblical worldview behind the evil in the world there lies the devil. The Greek word for the devil, *diabolos*, translates the Hebrew word *satan*. We are not told very much about the origins of Satan in the Bible. There is a hint that he may have been a fallen angel (Isaiah 14:12-23). He appears on a few occasions in the books of the Old Testament (Job 1; 1 Chronicles 21:1). He is not merely a force but is personal.

We are given a clearer picture of his activities in the New Testament. The devil is a personal spiritual being who is in active rebellion against God and has the leadership of many demons like himself. Paul tells us to take our 'stand against the devil's schemes. For our struggle is not against flesh and blood, but against the rulers, against the authorities . . . against the spiritual forces of evil in the heavenly realms' (Ephesians 6:11-12).

The devil and his angels, according to Paul, are not to be underestimated. They are cunning ('the devil's schemes' v. 11). They are powerful ('rulers', 'authorities' and 'forces' v. 12). They are evil ('forces of evil' v. 12). Therefore, we should not be surprised when we come under a powerful assault from the enemy.

WHY SHOULD WE BELIEVE IN THE DEVIL?

Why should we believe in the existence of the devil? Some say, 'Nowadays you can't believe in the devil.' However, there are very good reasons to believe in his existence.

First, it is biblical. That is not to say that the Bible concentrates on the devil. Satan is not mentioned very often in the Old Testament and it is only when we come to the New Testament that the doctrine is developed more fully. Jesus clearly believed in the existence of Satan and was tempted by him. He frequently cast out demons, freeing people from the forces of evil and sin in their lives, and gave his disciples authority to do the same. In the rest of the New Testament there are many references to the work of the devil (1 Peter 5:8-11; Ephesians 6:1-12).

Secondly, Christians down the ages have almost invariably believed in the existence of the devil. The early church theologians, the Reformers, the great evangelists like Wesley and Whitefield, and the overwhelming majority of men and women of God, knew that there were very real spiritual forces of evil around. As soon as we start to serve the Lord, his interest is aroused. 'The devil only tempts those souls that wish to abandon sin . . . the others belong to him: he has no need to tempt them.'[54]

Thirdly, common sense confirms the existence of the devil. Any kind of theology which ignores the existence of a personal devil has a great deal to explain: evil regimes, institutional torture and violence, mass murders, brutal rapes, large scale drug trafficking, terrorist atrocities, sexual and physical abuse of children, occult activity and satanic rituals. Who is behind all of this? There is a ditty which goes like this:

> Some say the devil's been,
> Some say the devil's gone,
> But simple people,
> like you and me,
> Would like to know,
> who carries the business on?

So Scripture, tradition and reason all point to the existence of the devil. This does not mean that we should become obsessed by him. As C. S. Lewis points out, 'There are two equal and opposite errors into which our race can fall about the devils. One is to disbelieve in their existence. The other is to believe, and to feel an excessive and unhealthy interest in them. They themselves are equally pleased by both errors and hail a materialist or a magician with the same delight.'[55]

As Michael Green has put it:

> Like any general who can persuade the opposition to underestimate him, Satan . . . must be enchanted at the present state of affairs which leaves him free to operate with the maximum of ease and efficiency, confident that nobody takes him seriously. The more he can do to encourage this doubt of his existence, the better. The more he can blind people's minds to the true state of affairs, the better his aims are furthered.[56]

Many fall into the opposite danger of having an excessive and unhealthy interest in him. There is a whole new interest in spiritualism, palm-reading, ouija boards, 'channelling' (consulting the dead), astrology, horoscopes, witchcraft and occult powers. Involvement in these things is expressly forbidden in Scripture (Deuteronomy 18:10; Leviticus 19:20ff; Galatians 5:19ff; Revelation 21:8; 22:15). If we have meddled in any of these things, we can be forgiven. We need to repent and destroy anything associated with that activity such as books, charms, videos and magazines (Acts 19:19).

Christians too can have an unhealthy interest in these things. A new Christian recently showed me a couple of supposedly Christian books where the whole emphasis was on the work of the enemy – with a lot of space devoted to speculation concerning the number of the beast in Revelation, and tying this in with credit cards! The intention was good, I am sure, but the focus on the work of the enemy seemed to me to be unhealthy. The Bible never has this kind of focus. The spotlight is always on God.

WHAT ARE THE DEVIL'S TACTICS?

The ultimate aim of Satan is to destroy every human being (John 10:10). He wants us to follow a path that leads to destruction. To that end, he tries to prevent anyone coming to faith in Jesus Christ. Paul tells us: 'The god of this age [the devil] has blinded the minds of unbelievers, so that they cannot see the light of the gospel of the glory of Christ, who is the image of God' (2 Corinthians 4:4).

So long as we are going along Satan's path and our eyes are blinded, we will probably be almost totally unaware of his tactics. Once we start walking along the path that leads to life and our eyes are opened to the truth, we become aware that we are under attack.

The initial line of attack is often in the area of doubt. We see this in the opening chapters of Genesis where the enemy, in the form of a serpent, says to Eve, 'Did God *really* say . . . ?' His opening move is to raise a doubt in her mind.

We see the same tactic in the temptation of Jesus. The devil comes to him and says, '*If* you are the Son of God . . .' (Matthew 4:3, italics mine). First, he raises doubts, then come the temptations. His tactics have not changed. He still raises doubts in our mind: 'Did God *really* say that such and such a course of action is wrong?' or, '*If* you are a Christian. . . .' He tries to undermine our confidence in what God has said and in our relationship with him. We need to recognise this source of many of our doubts.

Raising doubts was the precursor to the main attack on both Eve in the Garden of Eden and Jesus in the wilderness. In Genesis 3, we see an exposé of the way in which Satan, who is described as 'the tempter' (Matthew 4:2), so often works.

In Genesis 2:16-17, God gave Adam and Eve a far-reaching permission ('You are free to eat from any tree in the garden'), one prohibition ('But you must not eat from the tree of the knowledge of good and evil') and then warned them of the penalty if they disobeyed ('For when you eat of it you will surely die').

Satan ignores the wide scope of the permission and concentrates on the one prohibition – which he then exaggerates (Genesis 3:1). His tactics have not changed. He still ignores the permission. He ignores the fact that God has given us all things richly to enjoy (1 Timothy 6:17). He ignores the great blessing of walking in a relationship with God. He ignores the riches of Christian marriages and families, the security of a Christian home, the level of friendship that we can enjoy as Christians, and countless other things which God offers to those who know and love him. He does not tell us about these things. Instead he concentrates on a tiny unimaginative list of prohibitions of what Christians are not allowed to do – reminding us again and again that we can't get drunk, swear or be promiscuous. There are relatively few things that God does not allow us to do and there are very good reasons why he prohibits them.

Finally, he denies the penalty. He says, 'You will not surely die' (Genesis 3:4). He says, in effect, that it will not do you any harm to disobey God. He suggests to us that God is really a spoilsport, that God does not want the best for our lives and that we will miss out if we don't disobey. In fact the opposite is the case, as Adam and Eve found out. It is disobedience which causes us to miss out on so much of what God intended for us.

In the verses that follow, we see the consequences of disobeying God. First, there is shame and embarrassment. Adam and Eve felt exposed and began a cover-up operation (v. 7). How quickly would we want to leave the room if every action we had ever done was displayed on a screen, followed by a written list of every thought we had ever entertained? Deep down, we all feel ashamed and embarrassed by our sin. We don't want people to find us out. Sir Arthur Conan Doyle once played a practical joke on twelve men. They were all very well-known, respected and respectable men, regarded as pillars of the establishment. He sent each of them a telegram, with the same message in each: 'Flee at once. All is discovered.' Within twenty-four hours, they had all fled the country! Virtually all of us have something in our lives of which we are ashamed; something we would not want everyone to know about. We often put up barriers around us to avoid the possibility of being found out.

Next, Adam and Eve's friendship with God was broken. When they heard God coming, they hid (v. 8). Many people today shy away from God. They don't want to face up to the fact of the possibility of his existence. Like Adam they are afraid (v. 10). Some have a real fear of going to church or mixing with Christians. A couple in our congregation told me about a sixteen-stone rugby player from Australia whom they had invited to church. He got as far as the drive, then he started shaking in the car. He said, 'I can't go. I'm too frightened to go into the church.' He could not look God in the face. There was a separation between him and God, just as there was with Adam and Eve. God immediately started to try to draw them back into a relationship. He called out, 'Where are you?' (v. 9). He still does.

Then, there is a separation between Adam and Eve themselves. Adam blames Eve. Eve blames the devil. But they and we are responsible for our own sin. We cannot blame God or others or even the devil (James 1:13-15). We see this in our society today. When people turn away from God, they start fighting one another. We see the breakdown of relationships wherever we look: broken marriages, broken homes, broken relationships at work, civil war and war between nations.

Finally, we see in God's punishment of Adam and Eve (v. 14 onwards) that they were deceived by Satan. We see how his deception led Adam and Eve away from God into a path which, as Satan knew from the beginning, led to destruction.

We see that Satan is a deceiver, a destroyer, a tempter and one who raises doubts. He is also an accuser. The Hebrew word for Satan means 'accuser' or 'slanderer'. He accuses God before people. God gets the blame for everything. God, he says, is not to be trusted. Secondly, he accuses Christians before God (Revelation 12:10). He denies the power of the death of Jesus. He condemns us and makes us feel guilty – not for any particular sin, but with a general and vague feeling of guilt. In contrast, when the Holy Spirit draws attention to a sin, he identifies it so that we can turn from it.

Temptation is not the same thing as sin. Sometimes the devil puts a thought into our mind which we know is wrong. At that moment we have a choice whether to accept it or reject it. If we accept it, we are on the way towards sin. If we reject it, we do what Jesus did. He was 'tempted in every way, just as we are – yet was without sin' (Hebrews 4:15). When Satan put evil thoughts in his mind, he rejected them. But often before we have the chance to decide one way or the other, Satan accuses us. Within a split second he says, 'Look at you! Call yourself a Christian? What was that you were thinking about? You can't be a Christian. What a terrible thing to think!' He wants us to agree and say, 'Oh no! I can't be a Christian,' or, 'Oh no! I've blown it now, so it doesn't matter if I blow it a bit more!' We are on the way down, and this is his aim. The tactics are those of condemnation and accusation. If he can provoke guilt in us he knows the thought is: 'It doesn't really make any difference now if I do it or not. I have already failed.' So we do it and temptation becomes sin.

He wants failure to become a pattern in our lives. He knows that the more we fall into sin, the more sin will start to control our lives.

The first injection of heroin may not be enough to get a grip, but if you inject it day after day, month after month, year after year, it gets a grip and you become an addict. It has taken hold of you. If we fall into a pattern of doing things which we know to be wrong, these things grip our lives. We become addicted and we are on the path that Satan desires – the one that leads to destruction (Matthew 7:13).

WHAT IS OUR POSITION?

As Christians, God has rescued us from 'the dominion of darkness and brought us into the kingdom of the Son he loves' (Colossians 1:13). Before we were Christians, Paul says, we were in the dominion of darkness. Satan rules us and we were subject to sin, slavery, death and destruction. That is what the dominion of darkness is like.

Now, Paul says, we have been transferred from the kingdom of darkness to the kingdom of light. The moment we come to Christ we are transferred from darkness to light, and in the kingdom of light, Jesus is King. There is forgiveness, freedom, life and salvation. Once we have been transferred, we belong to someone else: to Jesus Christ and his kingdom.

In 1992 the Italian club Lazio paid £5.5 million for Paul Gascoigne to be transferred from Tottenham Hotspur to Lazio. Imagine that Gazza, while playing for Lazio, one day gets a phone-call from Terry Venables, his previous manager at Tottenham Hotspur, saying, 'Why weren't you at the practice this morning?' He would reply, 'I don't work for you any more. I have been transferred. I am working for another club' (or at least that is the gist of what he would say!).

In a far more wonderful way, we have been transferred from the kingdom of darkness where Satan is in charge, to the kingdom of God where Jesus is in charge. When Satan asks us to do his work our reply is, 'I don't belong to you any more.'

Satan is a conquered foe (Luke 10:17-20). On the cross Jesus 'disarmed the powers and authorities' and 'made a public spectacle of them, triumphing over them by the cross' (Colossians 2:15). Satan and all his minions were defeated at the cross, and that is why Satan and his demons are so frightened of the name of Jesus (Acts 16:18). They know they are defeated.

Jesus has freed us from guilt, so we don't need to be condemned. He has set us free from addictions. Jesus broke the power of these things and set us free. He broke the fear of death when he defeated death. With that, he set us free, potentially, from every fear. All these things – guilt, addiction and fear – belong to the kingdom of darkness. Jesus has transferred us to a new kingdom.

The cross was a great victory over Satan and his minions, and we now live in the time of the mopping-up operations. Although the enemy is not yet destroyed and is still capable of inflicting casualties, he is disarmed, defeated and demoralised. This is our position, and it is vital to realise the strength of the position we are in, due to the victory of Jesus on the cross for us.

HOW DO WE DEFEND OURSELVES?

Since the war is not over and Satan is not yet destroyed, we need to make sure that our defences are in order. Paul tells us to 'put on the full armour of God so that you can take your stand against the devil's schemes' (Ephesians 6:11). He then mentions six pieces of equipment which we need. Sometimes it is said, 'The secret of the Christian life is. . . .' But there is no one secret; we need *all* the armour.

First, we need the 'belt of truth' (v. 14). This probably means the foundation of Christian doctrine and truth. It means getting the whole Christian truth (or as much of it as one can) into one's system. We do this by reading the Bible, listening to sermons and talks, reading Christian books and listening to tapes. This will enable us to distinguish what is true and what are Satan's lies, for Satan is 'a liar and the father of lies' (John 8:44).

Next, we need the breastplate of righteousness (v. 14). This is the righteousness that comes from God through what Jesus has done for us on the cross. It enables us to be in a relationship with God and to live a righteous life. We need to resist the devil. The apostle James says, 'Resist the devil, and he will flee from you. Come near to God and he will come near to you' (James 4:7-8). We all fall from time to time. When we do, we need to get up quickly. We do this by telling God how sorry we are for what we have done, being as specific as possible (1 John 1:9). He then promises to restore his friendship with us.

Then, we also need the boots of the gospel of peace (v. 15). I understand this to mean a readiness to speak about the gospel of Jesus Christ. As John Wimber often said, 'It is hard to sit still and be good.' If we are constantly seeking opportunities to pass on the good news, we have an effective defence against the enemy. Once we declare our Christian faith to our families and at work, we strengthen our defence. It is hard, because we know that we are being watched to see if we live up to our faith. But it is a great incentive to do so.

The fourth piece of armour is the shield of faith (v. 16). With this, we 'can extinguish all the flaming arrows of the evil one'. Faith is the opposite of cynicism and scepticism which wreak havoc in many lives. One aspect of faith has been defined as 'taking a promise of God and daring to believe it'. Satan will throw his arrows of doubt to undermine us – but with the shield of faith we resist him.

Fifthly, Paul tells us to take the helmet of salvation (v. 17). As Bishop Westcott, Regius Professor of Divinity at Cambridge, once pointed out, there are three tenses of salvation. We have been saved from the penalty of sin. We are being saved from the power of sin. We shall be saved from the presence of sin. We need to grasp these great concepts in our mind; to know them so that we can answer the enemy's doubts and accusations.

Finally, we are to take 'the sword of the Spirit, which is the word of God' (v. 17). Probably here Paul is thinking of the Scriptures. Jesus used the Scriptures when Satan attacked. Each time Jesus replied with the word of God and in the end Satan had to leave. It is well worth learning verses from the Bible which we can use to see off the enemy and remind ourselves of the promises of God.

HOW DO WE ATTACK?

As we have already seen, Satan and his minions were defeated on the cross, and we are now involved in the final mopping-up operations before the return of Jesus. As Christians, we need not be afraid of Satan; he has a great deal to fear from the activity of Christians.

We are called to pray. We are involved in spiritual warfare, though 'the weapons we fight with are not the weapons of the world. On the contrary, they have divine power to demolish strongholds' (2 Corinthians 10:4). Prayer was a very high priority for Jesus, and it should be for us. In the words of the hymn, 'Satan trembles when he sees the weakest Christian on his knees.'

We are also called to action. Again, in the life of Jesus, prayer and action go hand in hand. Jesus proclaimed the kingdom of God, healed the sick and cast out demons. He commissioned his disciples to do the same. Later on we will look in more detail at what this means.

It is important to stress the greatness of God and the relative powerlessness of the enemy. We do not believe that there are two equal and opposite powers – God and Satan. That is not the biblical picture. God is the Creator of the universe. Satan is a part of his creation – a fallen part. He is a small part. Further, he is a defeated enemy and is about to be utterly wiped out when Jesus returns (Revelation 12:12).

In a superb picture in C. S. Lewis' book *The Great Divorce*, where he speaks about hell as the place where Satan and his demons operate, a man has arrived in heaven and is being shown round by his 'teacher'. He goes down on hands and knees, takes a blade of grass and, using the thin end as a pointer, he eventually finds a tiny crack in the soil in which is concealed the whole of hell:

'Do you mean then that Hell – all that infinite empty town – is down in some little crack like this?'

'Yes. All Hell is smaller than one pebble of your earthly world: but it is smaller than one atom of *this* world, the Real World. Look at yon butterfly. If it swallowed all Hell, Hell would not be big enough to do it any harm or to have any taste.'

'It seems big enough when you are in it, Sir.'

'And yet all loneliness, angers, hatreds, envies and itchings that it contains, if rolled into one single experience and put into the scale against the least moment of the joy that is felt by the least in Heaven, would have no weight that could be registered at all. Bad cannot succeed even in being bad as truly as good is good. If all Hell's miseries together entered the consciousness of yon wee yellow bird on the bough there, they would be swallowed up without trace, as if one drop of ink had been dropped into that Great Ocean to which your terrestrial Pacific itself is only a molecule.'[57]

12

Why and How Should I Tell Others?

Why should we talk about our Christian faith? Isn't it a private matter? Isn't the best sort of Christian the one who just lives the Christian life? Sometimes people say to me, 'I know someone [usually their mother or their aunt] who is a Christian. They have a really strong faith – but they do not talk about it. Isn't that the highest form of Christianity?'

The short answer is that someone must have told them about the Christian faith. The slightly longer answer is that there are good reasons for telling others about Jesus. First, it is a command of Jesus himself. Tom Forrest, the Roman Catholic priest who first suggested to the Pope the idea of calling the 1990s 'The Decade of Evangelism', points out that the word 'go' appears 1,514 times in the Bible (RSV), 233 times in the New Testament and 54 times in Matthew's Gospel. Jesus tells us to 'go':

'Go to the lost sheep . . .'
'Go and tell John . . .'
'Go and invite all you meet . . .'
'Go and make disciples . . .'

Indeed, these are the last recorded words of Jesus in Matthew's Gospel:

> Then Jesus came to them and said, 'All authority in heaven and on earth has been given to me. Therefore go and make disciples of all nations, baptising them in the name of the Father and of the Son and of the Holy Spirit, and teaching them to obey everything I have commanded you. And surely I will be with you always, to the very end of the age' (Matthew 28:18-20).

Secondly, we tell people because there is a desperate need for people to hear the good news of Jesus Christ. If we were in the Sahara Desert and had discovered an oasis, it would be extremely selfish not to tell the people around us who were thirsty where their thirst could be satisfied. Jesus is the only One who can satisfy the thirsty hearts of men and women. Often the recognition of this thirst comes from surprising sources. The singer, Sinead O'Connor, said in an interview: 'As a race we feel empty. This is because our spirituality has been wiped out and we don't know how to express ourselves. As a result we're encouraged to fill that gap with alcohol, drugs, sex or money. People out there are screaming for the truth.'

Thirdly, we tell others because, having discovered the good news ourselves, we feel an urgent desire to pass it on. If we have received good news we want to tell others. When our first child was born, my wife Pippa gave me a list of about ten people to ring. The first person I rang was her mother. I told her that we had a son and that he and Pippa were well. I then tried ringing my mother, but the phone was engaged. The third person on the list was Pippa's sister. By the time I had telephoned her she had already heard the news from Pippa's mother and so had all the others on the list. My mother's phone had been engaged because Pippa's mother was ringing her with the news. Good news travels fast. I did not need to implore Pippa's mother to pass on the message. She was bursting to tell them all. When we appreciate what good news the gospel is, we shall be bursting to tell others.

But how do we go about telling others? It seems to me that there are two opposite dangers. First, there is the danger of insensitivity. When I first became a Christian I fell into this. I was so excited about what had happened that I longed for everyone else to follow suit. After I had been a Christian for a few days I went to a party, determined to tell everyone. I saw a friend dancing and decided the first step was to make her realise her need. So I went up to her and said, 'You look awful. You really need Jesus.' She thought that I had gone mad. It was not the most effective way of telling someone the good news! (However, she did later become a Christian – quite independently of me, and she is now my wife!)

The next party I went to I decided to go well equipped. So I got hold of a number of booklets, Christian books on various issues and a New Testament. I stuffed them into every pocket I could find. Somehow I managed to find a girl who was willing to dance with me. It was hard going with so many books in my pocket, so I asked if we could sit down. I soon brought the subject round to Christianity. For every question she asked, I was able to produce a book from my pocket on exactly that subject. Eventually she went away with an armful of books. The next day she was going to France and was reading one of the books I had given her on the boat. Suddenly she understood the truth of what Jesus had done for her and, turning to her neighbour, she said, 'I have just become a Christian.' She died in a riding accident at the age of twenty-one. It was wonderful that she had come to Christ before she died – even though I don't think I went about it in quite the right way.

If we charge around like a bull in a china shop, sooner or later we get hurt. Even if we approach the subject sensitively, we may still get hurt. When we do, we tend to withdraw. Certainly this was my experience. After a few years, I moved from the danger of insensitivity and fell into the opposite danger of fear. There was a time (ironically it was when I was at theological college) when I became fearful of even talking about Jesus to those who were not Christians. On one occasion, a group of us went from the college to a parish mission on the outskirts of Liverpool, to tell people the good news. Each night we had supper with different people from the parish. One night a friend of mine called Rupert and I were sent to supper with a couple who were on the fringe of the church (or, to be more accurate, the wife was on the fringe and the husband was not a churchgoer). Halfway through the main course the husband asked me what we were doing up there. I stumbled, stammered, hesitated and prevaricated. He kept on repeating the question. Eventually Rupert said straight out, 'We have come here to tell people about Jesus.' I felt deeply embarrassed and hoped the ground would swallow us all up! I realised how frozen with fear I had become and that I was afraid even to take the name of Jesus on my lips.

In order to avoid these dangers of insensitivity and fear, we need to realise that telling others about Jesus arises out of our own relationship with God. It is a natural part of that relationship. As we walk with God, it should be quite natural for us to talk to people about that relationship in co-operation with the Spirit of God.

I find it helpful to think of this subject under five headings – all beginning with the letter 'p' – presence, persuasion, proclamation, power and prayer.

PRESENCE

Jesus said to his disciples:

> You are the salt of the earth. But if the salt loses its saltiness, how can it be made salty again? It is no longer good for anything, except to be thrown out and trampled under foot. You are the light of the world. A city on a hill cannot be hidden. Neither do people light a lamp and put it under a bowl. Instead they put it on its stand, and it gives light to everyone in the house. In the same way, let your light shine before others, that they may see your good deeds and praise your Father in heaven (Matthew 5:13-16).

Jesus calls us to have a wide-ranging influence ('salt of the *earth*' and 'the light of the *world*'). In order to exercise this influence, we need to be 'in the world' (at work, in our neighbourhood and among our family and friends) and not to withdraw into what John Stott calls our 'elegant little ecclesiastical salt cellars'. Yet we are called to be different – to live a radically different lifestyle from the world, so that we may be effective as salt and light in it.

We are called first to be salt. In centuries before refrigeration was invented salt was used to keep meat wholesome and to prevent decay. We are called as Christians to stop society going bad. We do this by our words, as we speak out about moral standards and moral issues, and as we use our influence to bring about God's standards in society around us. We do it by our deeds as we play our part as citizens, aiming to create better social structures, working for justice, freedom and dignity for the individual, and by helping to abolish discrimination. We do it also by our social action to help those who are casualties of our society. To this end, some Christians are called to get involved in local or national politics. Others are called to spend their lives like Mother Teresa and Jackie Pullinger 'ministering *with* the poor' (to use Jackie Pullinger's expression). All of us are called to play a part in this to a greater or lesser extent.

Secondly, Jesus calls us to be light – to allow the light of Christ to shine through us. We do this by what Jesus calls 'your good deeds' – everything that we do or say because we are Christians. They can be summarised as 'loving our neighbour as ourselves'.

Living out the Christian life is the most appropriate way of passing on the good news to those who live in very close proximity to us. This certainly applies to our family, colleagues at work and flatmates. If they know we are Christians, that fact alone puts them under a degree of pressure. To be continually speaking about our faith may backfire. They are more likely to be affected by genuine love and concern. At work people should notice our consistency, honesty, truthfulness, hard work, reliability, avoidance of gossip and desire to encourage other people. At home, parents, family and flatmates will be influenced by our service to others, our patience and our kindness, far more than by our words.

This is of great importance if one's husband or wife is not a Christian. Peter encouraged Christian wives that if any of them have husbands who 'do not believe the word, they may be won over *without talk* by the behaviour of their wives, when they see the purity and reverence of your lives' (1 Peter 3:1, italics mine).

Bruce and Geraldine Streather were married in December 1973. When Geraldine came to Christ in 1981, Bruce was not remotely interested. Bruce was a busy lawyer and a very keen golfer: he used to play most weekends. He never came to church.

For ten years Geraldine prayed for him and lived out the Christian life in front of him. She did not put any pressure on him and did not engage in any arguments about it. Over the years, Bruce was struck by her extraordinary kindness and consideration, especially to his mother whose cancer and related illnesses made her increasingly difficult. Eventually, in 1991, she invited him to come to an Alpha supper. Bruce came, and decided to come on the following Alpha course.

Geraldine wrote to me afterwards saying, 'I cried all the way home and prayed, telling God that as I had got Bruce to Alpha, he must do the rest. When Bruce returned from the first night of the course, I only asked him if he had enjoyed himself.'

On week seven of the course, Bruce gave his life to Christ and by the end he was the most enthusiastic Christian one could ever meet. I asked Geraldine what it was like living with him now. She replied, 'It's a bit like living with Billy Graham!'

Her letter continued: 'He tells everyone about Jesus. Instead of trying not to mention Christianity in front of friends when Bruce was there, in case it harmed our marriage, at every dinner party he talks to people about God and I am left at the other end listening to what he is saying. It seems that all my prayers have been answered. Last March I told God that I was fed up with Bruce not being a Christian. I told him I didn't care what happened to our house or money as long as Bruce became a Christian. Life will never be the same again – thank God for that.'

Nevertheless, being 'lights in the world' does not just involve our lifestyle. It also involves our lips. Our family, our flatmates and our colleagues will eventually ask questions about our faith. It is often better to wait until they do. If we are asked, we should always be prepared to give an answer. Peter writes: 'Always be prepared to give an answer to everyone who asks you to give the reason for the hope that you have. But do this with gentleness and respect' (1 Peter 3:15).

When we do get opportunities to speak, how do we go about it?

PERSUASION

Many people today have objections to the Christian faith or, at least, questions which they want answered before they are ready to come to faith in Christ. They need to be persuaded about the truth. Paul was willing to try to persuade people. He regarded it as his duty out of love for them: 'Since, then, we know what it is to fear the Lord, we try to *persuade* people' (2 Corinthians 5:11, italics mine).

When he went to Thessalonica he 'reasoned', 'explained' and 'proved' from the Scriptures that the Christ had to suffer and rise from the dead: '. . . some of the Jews were persuaded . . .' (Acts 17:4). In Corinth, while working on tents during the week, 'every Sabbath he reasoned in the synagogue, trying to persuade Jews and Greeks' (Acts 18:4).

During the course of conversations about the Christian faith, objections will often be raised and we need to be equipped to deal with these. On one occasion, Jesus was talking to a woman about the mess her life was in (John 4). Then he offered her eternal life. At that moment she raised a theological question about places of worship. He answered it, but quickly brought the conversation back to the essential issue. This is a good example for us to follow.

Usually when people raise theological questions and objections, they are genuinely looking for the answers. The most common questions which I get asked are, 'Why does God allow suffering?' and, 'What about other religions?' But there are a whole range of other questions. These may be serious, and may require a serious answer. Sometimes, however, these questions can be a smokescreen to avoid the real issue. Such people are put off becoming Christians, not by the theological objections, but by the moral ones. They are not willing to give their lives to Christ for fear of the change of lifestyle that Christianity will involve.

On the mission which I mentioned earlier in the chapter, Rupert and I went to speak at a meeting about our Christian faith. After we had spoken, a university lecturer raised a large number of questions and objections. I didn't know where to begin to answer them all. Rupert simply asked, 'If we could answer all your questions satisfactorily, would you become a Christian?' He replied, very honestly, 'No.' So there didn't seem a great deal of point in answering what for him were purely academic enquiries. But when the questions are genuine, reasoning, explaining and proving form an important part of telling others about Jesus.

PROCLAMATION

The heart of telling others is the proclamation of the good news of Jesus Christ. It is announcing, communicating and proclaiming the Christian faith to those outside the faith. There are many ways in which this can be done. One of the most effective ways is bringing people to hear the gospel explained by someone else. This can often be more advisable, especially in the early stages of our Christian lives, than trying to explain the gospel ourselves.

Many who come to faith in Christ have lots of friends who have little or no connection with the church. This provides an excellent opportunity to say to these friends, as Jesus did on one occasion, 'Come . . . and you will see' (John 1:39). A woman in her twenties recently became a Christian and started coming to church in London. At weekends, however, she would stay with her parents in Wiltshire, and she then insisted on leaving them at 3 pm on Sunday afternoon in order to be in time for church. One Sunday evening she got stuck in a bad traffic jam on the Hammersmith flyover and could not get to the evening service. She was so upset that she burst into tears. She went round to see some friends, who did not even know she had become a Christian. They asked her what was wrong. She answered through the tears, 'I've missed church.' They were totally mystified. The next Sunday they all came to see what they were missing! One of them came to Christ very shortly afterwards.

There is no greater privilege and no greater joy than enabling someone to find out about Jesus Christ. The former Archbishop of Canterbury, William Temple, wrote his commentary on John's Gospel while on his knees, asking God to speak to his heart. When he came to the words, 'And he [Andrew] brought Simon to Jesus' (John 1:42), he wrote a short but momentous sentence: 'The greatest service that one man can render another.'

We don't hear much more about Andrew except that he was always bringing people to Jesus (John 6:8; 12:22). But Simon Peter his brother went on to be one of the greatest influences in the history of Christianity. We cannot all be Simon Peters, but we can all do what Andrew did – we can bring someone to Jesus.

Albert McMakin was a twenty-four-year-old farmer who had recently come to faith in Christ. He was so full of enthusiasm that he filled a truck with people and took them to a meeting to hear about Jesus. There was a good-looking farmer's son whom he was especially keen to get to a meeting, but this young man was hard to persuade – he was busy falling in and out of love with different girls, and did not seem to be attracted to Christianity. Eventually, Albert McMakin managed to persuade him to come by asking him to drive the truck. When they arrived, Albert's guest decided to go in and was 'spellbound' and began to have thoughts he had never known before. He went back again and again until one night, he went forward and gave his life to Jesus Christ. That man, the driver of the truck, was Billy Graham. The year was 1934. Since then Billy Graham has led thousands to faith in Jesus Christ. We cannot all be like Billy Graham, but we can all be like Albert McMakin – we can all bring our friends to Jesus.

Sometimes we are given the opportunity to explain the gospel ourselves. One good way of doing this is to tell the story of what has happened to us. We see a biblical model in Paul's testimony in Acts 26:9-23. It falls into three parts: he speaks about what he was like before (vv. 9-11), what it meant to meet Jesus (vv. 12-15) and what it has meant for him since (vv. 19-23). When explaining what someone has to do to become a Christian, a framework can be helpful. There are many different ways of presenting the gospel. I have set out the method I use in a booklet called *Why Jesus?*. I then lead people in the prayer which you will find at the end of Chapter 4 of *this* book.

One man in our church told me recently about how he had come to Christ. He was going through difficulties in his business and had to go to the United States on a business trip. He was not feeling very happy as he rode in a taxi to the airport. On the dashboard of the taxi he noticed pictures of the taxi driver's children. He could not see the face of the driver, but he asked him about his family. He felt great love coming from the man. As the conversation went on, the taxi driver said to him, 'I sense that you are not happy. If you believe in Christ it makes all the difference.'

The businessman said to me, 'Here was a man speaking with authority. I thought I was the one in authority. After all, I was paying.' The taxi driver said to him eventually, 'Don't you think it's time you settled all this by accepting Christ?' They arrived at the airport. For the first time the taxi driver turned round and the businessman saw his face – it was full of kindness. He said to him, 'Why don't we pray? If you want Christ in your life, ask him.' They prayed together and the driver gave him a booklet about the Christian faith. The taxi driver was a modest unassuming person who was there one moment and gone the next, but he had taken the opportunity to proclaim the good news of Jesus Christ. This changed the whole course of a man's life.

POWER

In the New Testament the proclamation of the gospel is often accompanied by a demonstration of the power of God. Jesus came proclaiming: 'The kingdom of God is near. Repent and believe the good news!' (Mark 1:15). Jesus went on to demonstrate the power of the gospel by the expulsion of evil (Mark 1:21-28) and by healing the sick (Mark 1:29-34, 40-45).

Jesus told his disciples to do what he had been doing. He told them to do the works of the kingdom – 'to heal the sick who are there' and to proclaim the good news – and to tell them, 'The kingdom of God is near you' (Luke 10:9). As we read on in the Gospels and Acts we see that that is what they did. Paul wrote to the Thessalonians: 'Our gospel came to you not simply with words, but also with power' (1 Thessalonians 1:5).

Proclamation and demonstration go hand in hand. Often one leads to the other. On one occasion Peter and John were on their way to church. Outside was a man crippled from birth. He had been sitting there for years. He asked for money. Peter said, in effect, 'I am sorry. I haven't got any money, but I will give you what I have. In the name of Jesus Christ of Nazareth, walk.' He took his hand and helped him up. Instantly, he jumped to his feet and began to walk. When he realised he was healed, he leapt and jumped and praised God (Acts 3:1-10).

Everyone knew that this man had been crippled for years, and a huge crowd gathered around. After the demonstration of the power of God came the proclamation of the gospel. People were asking, 'How did this happen?' Peter was able to tell them all about Jesus: 'It is Jesus' name and the faith that comes through him that has given this complete healing to him, as you can all see' (Acts 3:16). In the next chapter we shall examine this area in more detail by looking at the nature of the kingdom of God and the place of healing in it.

PRAYER

We have already seen the importance that prayer had in the life of Jesus. While he was proclaiming and demonstrating the gospel he was also praying (Mark 1:35-37). Prayer is essential in the area of telling others the good news.

We need to pray for blind eyes to be opened. Many people are blinded to the gospel (2 Corinthians 4:4). They can see physically, but they cannot see the spiritual world. We need to pray that the Spirit of God will open the eyes of the blind so that they can understand the truth about Jesus.

Most of us find, when we come to faith in Christ, that there has been somebody praying for us. It may be a member of the family, a godparent or a friend. There will be somebody, I suspect, in nearly every case who has been praying that our eyes will be opened to see the truth. James Hudson Taylor, who founded the China Inland Mission, influenced millions for Jesus Christ. He was brought up in Yorkshire and became a rebellious teenager. One day, when his mother was away and his sister was out, he picked up a Christian book, intending to read the story and skip the moral. He curled up in the barn behind the house and began to read.

As he read, he was struck by the phrase 'the finished work of Christ'. He thought Christianity to be a dreary struggle to pay off bad debts with good. He had long since abandoned the struggle. He owed too much. He sought simply to have a good time. This phrase broke open his mind to a sudden certainty that Christ, by his death on the cross, had already discharged this debt of sins: 'And with this dawned the joyful conviction, as light was flashed into my soul by the Holy Spirit, that there was nothing in the world to be done but to fall down on one's knees and accepting this Saviour and His Salvation, to praise Him for evermore.' No Luther, Bunyan or Wesley had a more complete sense of the rolling away of his burden, of light dismissing darkness, of rebirth and the close friendship of Christ, than did Hudson Taylor on that June afternoon in 1849 at the age of seventeen.

Ten days later his mother came home. He ran to the door 'to tell her I had such glad news to give'. She replied as she hugged him, 'I know, my boy. I have been rejoicing for a fortnight in the glad tidings you have to tell me.' Hudson was amazed. She had been eighty miles away, and on the very day of the incident in the barn she had felt such an overwhelming desire to pray for Hudson that she had spent hours on her knees, and had arisen with the unshakeable conviction that her prayers had been answered. He never forgot the importance of prayer.[58]

When a friend of mine, Ric, became a Christian he rang a friend whom he knew to be a Christian as well, and told him what had happened. The friend replied, 'I have been praying for you for four years.' Ric then started to pray for one of his own friends, and within ten weeks he too became a Christian.

We need to pray for our friends. We also need to pray for ourselves. When we talk to people about Jesus, we may sometimes get a negative reaction. The temptation at that moment is to give up. When Peter and John healed the crippled man and proclaimed the gospel, they were arrested and threatened with dire consequences should they continue. At times, they got a decidedly negative reaction; but they did not give up. Rather, they prayed – not for protection, but for boldness in preaching the gospel and for God to perform more signs and wonders through the name of Jesus (Acts 4:29-31).

It is vital for all of us as Christians to persevere in telling others about Jesus – by our presence, persuasion, proclamation, power and prayer. If we do, over the course of a lifetime we shall see many lives changed.

During the war a man was shot and lay dying in the trenches. A friend leaned over to him and said, 'Is there anything I can do for you?'

He replied, 'No, I am dying.'

'Is there anyone I can send a message to for you?'

'Yes, you can send a message to this man at this address. Tell him that in my last minutes what he taught me as a child is helping me to die.'

The man was his old Sunday school teacher. When the message got back to him, he said, 'God forgive me. I gave up Sunday school teaching years ago because I thought I was getting nowhere. I thought it was no use.'

When we tell people about Jesus, it is never 'no use'. For the gospel 'is the power of God for the salvation of everyone who believes' (Romans 1:16).

13

Does God Heal Today?

A few years ago, a Japanese girl asked myself and my wife to pray for her back problem to be healed. We placed our hands on her and asked God to heal her. Thereafter, I tried to avoid bumping into her because I was not sure how to explain to her why she had not been healed. One day she came round the corner and I could not avoid her. I thought it only polite to ask the dreaded question, 'How is your back?'

'Oh,' she replied, 'it was completely healed after you prayed for it.'

I don't know why I was so surprised, but I was.

When John Wimber came to our church with a team from his church (the Vineyard Christian Fellowship), he preached one Sunday on the subject of healing. On Monday he came to a gathering of leaders. There were about sixty or seventy of us in the room and he spoke again about healing. We had heard talks on healing before, and felt quite happy about what he said on the subject. That was until he said that we were going to break for coffee and then have a 'workshop'. We were now on unfamiliar ground. John Wimber said that his team had had some twelve 'words of knowledge' about the people in the room. He told us that by a 'word of knowledge' (1 Corinthians 12:8) he meant a supernatural revelation of facts concerning a person or a situation, which is not learned by the efforts of the natural mind, but is made known by the Spirit of God. This may be in the form of a picture, a word seen or heard in the mind, or a feeling experienced physically. He then gave a whole list of them and said that he was going to invite people to come forward to be prayed for. I, for one, was most sceptical about the whole event.

However, as one by one the people responded to some of the quite detailed descriptions (my recollection is that one of them was for 'a man who had injured his back chopping wood when he was fourteen'), the level of faith in the room began to rise. Every word of knowledge was responded to. One of them concerned sterility. We all knew each other well and felt sure that this was not applicable to anyone in the group. However, a girl who had been unable to conceive, bravely went forward. She was prayed for and had her first of five children exactly nine months later!

My attitude during that evening reflects the fear and scepticism many of us in the twenty-first century bring to the subject of healing. I decided to reread the Bible to try to understand what it said about healing. Of course, God heals with the co-operation of doctors, nurses and the whole medical profession. But the more I have looked, the more convinced I am that we should also expect God to heal miraculously today.

HEALING IN THE BIBLE

In the Old Testament we find God's promises to bring healing and health to his people if they obey him (eg, Exodus 23:25-26; Deuteronomy 28; Psalm 41). Indeed, it is in his character to heal, for he says, 'I am the Lord who heals you' (Exodus 15:26). We also find several examples of miraculous healing (eg, 1 Kings 13:6;

2 Kings 4:8-37; Isaiah 38).

One of the most striking examples is the healing of Naaman, the commander of the army of the King of Aram, who had leprosy. God healed him after he had reluctantly dipped himself seven times in the River Jordan. 'His flesh was restored and became clean like that of a young boy' (2 Kings 5:14), and he recognised the God of Israel to be the only true God. Elisha, who had instructed him, refused the payment which Naaman offered (although his servant Gehazi made the fatal mistake of trying, deceitfully, to get money for himself as a result of the healing). We see, first, from this story that healing can have a remarkable effect on a person's life – not just physically, but also in their relationship with God. Healing and faith can go hand in hand. Secondly, if God acted in this way in the Old Testament, when there were only glimpses of the kingdom of God and the outpouring of the Spirit, we can confidently expect that he will do so, even more, now that Jesus has inaugurated the kingdom of God and the age of the Spirit.

The first recorded words of Jesus in Mark's Gospel are, 'The time has come . . . The kingdom of God is near. Repent and believe the good news!' (Mark 1:15). The theme of the kingdom of God is central to the ministry of Jesus. The expressions 'the kingdom of God' and 'the kingdom of heaven' are used more than eighty-two times, although the latter is confined to Matthew's Gospel. The two terms are synonymous. 'Heaven' was a common Jewish expression for referring to God without mentioning the divine name. The Jewish background to Matthew's Gospel, as opposed to the Gentile orientation of Luke and Mark, probably explains the different use.

The Greek word for 'kingdom', *basileia*, is a translation of the Aramaic *malkuth*, which was in all probability the expression that Jesus used. It means not only 'kingdom' in the sense of a political or geographical realm, but also carries the notion of activity – the activity of ruling or reigning. Thus 'the kingdom of God' means 'the rule and reign of God'.

In the teaching of Jesus, the kingdom of God has a future aspect which will only be fulfilled with a decisive event at 'the end of the age' (Matthew 13:49). For example, in one of the parables of the kingdom, he speaks of a coming harvest at the end of the age when 'the Son of Man . . . will weed out of his kingdom everything that causes sin and all who do evil . . . Then the righteous will shine like the sun in the kingdom of their Father' (Matthew 13:24-43). The end of the age will come when Jesus returns. When he came the first time, he came in weakness; when he returns, he will come 'with power and great glory' (Matthew 24:30).

History is moving towards this climax with the glorious coming of Jesus Christ (Matthew 25:31). In all, there are over 300 references in the New Testament to the second coming of Christ. When he returns it will be obvious to all. History, as we know it, will end. There will be a universal resurrection and a Day of Judgement. For some (those who reject Christ), it will be a day of destruction (2 Thessalonians 1:8-9); for others, it will be a day of receiving their inheritance in the kingdom of God (Matthew 25:34). There will be a new heaven and a new earth (2 Peter 3:13; Revelation 21:1). Jesus himself will be there (Revelation 21:22-23) and so will all who love and obey him. It will be a place of intense happiness which goes on for ever (1 Corinthians 2:9). We shall have new bodies which are imperishable and glorious (1 Corinthians 15:42-43). There will be no more death or mourning or crying or pain (Revelation 21:4). All who believe will be totally healed on that day.

On the other hand, there is a present aspect to the kingdom of God in the teaching and activity of Jesus. We see the signs, the dawning, the budding of the approaching kingdom. Jesus told the Pharisees, 'The kingdom of God is among you' (Luke 17:20-21).

In his parable of the hidden treasure and the pearl (Matthew 13:44-46), Jesus suggests that the kingdom is something which can be discovered and experienced in this age. Throughout the Gospels it is clear that Jesus saw his ministry as the fulfilment of the Old Testament promises in history. In the synagogue at Nazareth, Jesus read the prophecy from Isaiah 61:1-2 and asserted, 'Today this scripture is fulfilled in your hearing' (Luke 4:21). He went on to demonstrate this present reality of the kingdom by all that he did during his ministry, in the forgiveness of sins, the suppression of evil and the healing of the sick.

The kingdom is both 'now' and 'not yet'. The Jewish expectation was that the Messiah would immediately inaugurate a completed kingdom, as shown in the diagram below:

THIS AGE | AGE TO COME

Jesus' teaching was a modification of this and can be summarised in the diagram below:

The age to come realised in principle — AGE TO COME

Second coming of Jesus

The period in which we now live

First coming of Jesus

THIS AGE

We live between the times, when the age to come has broken into history. The old age goes on, but the powers of the new age have erupted into this age. The future kingdom has broken into history. Jesus preached the kingdom of God. He also demonstrated its breaking into history by healing the sick, raising the dead and driving out demons.

A quarter of the Gospels is concerned with healing. Although Jesus did not heal all in Judea who were sick, we often read of him healing either individuals or groups of people (eg, Matthew 4:23; 9:35; Mark 6:56; Luke 4:40; 6:19; 9:11). It was part of the normal activity of the kingdom.

Not only did he do this himself, but he commissioned his disciples to do the same. First, he commissioned the twelve. This is clearly set out in Matthew's Gospel. Matthew tells us that 'Jesus went throughout Galilee, teaching in their synagogues, preaching the good news of the kingdom, and healing every disease and sickness among the people' (Matthew 4:23). He then gives some of the teaching and preaching of Jesus in Matthew 5–7 (the Sermon on the Mount), then nine miracles (mainly of healing) and he concludes with an almost exact repetition of Matthew 4:23: 'Jesus went through all the towns and villages, teaching in their synagogues, preaching the good news of the kingdom and healing every kind of disease and sickness' (Matthew 9:35). Matthew is using a literary device of repetition known as an *inclusio*, which was used instead of punctuation and the breaking up of the text with paragraphs to indicate the beginning and end of a section. Having shown what Jesus himself did, Matthew tells us that Jesus then sent the twelve out to do the same. He told them to go out and preach the same message: '"The kingdom of heaven is near." Heal the sick, raise the dead, cleanse those who have leprosy, drive out demons . . .' (Matthew 10:8).

Nor was it only the twelve to whom he gave this commission.

There was also a further group of seventy-two whom he appointed. He told them to go out and 'heal the sick . . . and tell them, "The kingdom of God is near you"' (Luke 10:9). They returned with joy and said, 'Lord, even the demons submit to us in your name' (v. 17).

Nor were his commissions confined to the twelve and the seventy-two. Jesus expected *all* his disciples to do the same. He told his disciples to 'go and make disciples of all nations . . . teaching them to obey *everything* I have commanded you' (Matthew 28:18-20, italics mine). He did not say, 'Everything except, of course, the healing bit.'

We find the same in the longer ending of Mark's Gospel (which is, at least, very good evidence of what the early church understood Jesus' commission to be). Jesus said, '"Go into all the world and preach the good news to all creation . . . and these signs will accompany *those who believe*: In my name they will drive out demons . . . they will place their hands on sick people, and they will get well" . . . Then the disciples went out and preached everywhere, and the Lord worked with them and confirmed his word by the signs that accompanied it' (Mark 16:15-20, italics mine). Jesus says, 'These signs will accompany *those who believe*' – that is to say those 'who believe' in Jesus Christ, which means all Christians.

We find the same in John's Gospel. Jesus said, in the context of miracles, 'Anyone who has faith in me will do what I have been doing. He will do even greater things than these, because I am going to the Father' (John 14:12). Clearly no one has performed miracles of greater quality than Jesus, but there has been a greater quantity since Jesus returned to the Father. He has not ceased to perform miracles, but he now uses weak and imperfect human beings. Again it is 'anyone who has faith in me'. That is you and me. These commands and promises are not restricted anywhere to a special category of Christians.

Jesus healed; he told his disciples to do the same and they did so.

In the Book of Acts we see the working out of this commission. The disciples continued to preach and teach, but also to heal the sick, raise the dead and cast out demons (Acts 3:1-10; 4:12; 5:12-16; 8:5-13; 9:32-43; 14:3, 8-10; 19:11-12; 20:9-12; 28:8-9). It is clear from 1 Corinthians 12–14 that Paul did not believe that such abilities were confined to the apostles. Likewise, the writer to the Hebrews says that God testified to his message by 'signs, wonders and various miracles, and gifts of the Holy Spirit' (Hebrews 2:4).

Nowhere in the Bible does it say that healing was confined to any particular period of history. On the contrary, healing is one of the signs of the kingdom which was inaugurated by Jesus Christ and continues to this day. We should expect God to continue to heal miraculously today as part of his kingdom activity.

HEALING IN CHURCH HISTORY

In her book *Christian Healing* Evelyn Frost examined in detail passages of early church writers, such as Quadratus, Justin Martyr, Theophilus of Antioch, Irenaeus, Tertullian and Origen, and concluded that healing formed a normal part of the activity of the early church.

Irenaeus (c. 130-c. 200) who was Bishop of Lyons and one of the theologians of the early church wrote:

> Those who are in truth his disciples, receiving grace from him, do in his name perform [miracles], so as to promote the welfare of other men, according to the gift which each one has received from him. For some do certainly and truly drive out devils, so that those who have thus been cleansed from evil spirits frequently both believe [in Christ], and join themselves to the church. Others have foreknowledge of things to come: they see visions, and utter prophetic expressions.

Others still, heal the sick by laying their hands upon them and they are made whole. Yea, moreover, as I have said, the dead have been raised up, and remain among us for many years.[59]

Origen (c. 185-c. 254), another theologian, biblical scholar and writer of the early church, said of Christians: 'They expel evil spirits, and perform many cures, and foresee certain events . . . the name of Jesus . . . can take away diseases.'

Two hundred years later there was still an expectation that God would heal people directly. Augustine of Hippo (AD 354-430), whom many regard as the greatest theologian of the first four centuries, says in his book *The City of God* that '*even now* miracles are wrought in the name of Christ'. He cites the example of a blind man's sight restored in Milan, when he was there. He then describes the cure of a man he was staying with, called Innocentius. He was being treated by the doctors for fistulae, of which he had 'a large number intricately seated in the rectum'! He had undergone one very painful operation. It was not thought that he would survive another operation. While they were praying for him he was cast down to the ground as if someone had hurled him violently to the earth, groaning and sobbing, his whole body shaking so that he could not speak. The dreaded day for the next operation came. 'The surgeons arrived . . . the frightful instruments are produced . . . the part is bared; the surgeon . . . with knife in hand, eagerly looks for the sinus that is to be cut. He searches for it with his eyes; he feels for it with his finger; he applies every kind of scrutiny.' He found a perfectly healed wound. 'No words of mine can describe the joy, and praise, and thanksgiving to the merciful and almighty God which was poured from the lips of all, with tears and gladness. Let the scene be imagined rather than described!'

Next he described the healing of Innocentia – a devout woman of the highest rank in the state – who was healed of what the doctors described as incurable breast cancer. The doctor was curious to find out how she had been healed. When she told him that Jesus had healed her, he was furious and said, 'I thought you would make some great discovery to me.' She, shuddering at the indifference, quickly replied, 'What great thing was it for Christ to heal a cancer, who raised one who had been four days dead?'

He goes on to tell of a doctor with gout who was healed in the 'very act of baptism' and an old comedian who was also cured at baptism, not only of paralysis, but also of a hernia. Augustine says he knows of so many miraculous healings that he says at one point, 'What am I to do? I am so pressed by the promise of finishing this work, that I cannot record all the miracles I know . . . even now, therefore many miracles are wrought, the same God, who wrought those we read of, still performing them, by whom he will and as he will.'

All the way through church history God has continued to heal people directly. There has never been a time when healing has died out – right up to the present day.

Edward Gibbon, the English rationalist, historian and scholar, best known as the author of *The History of the Decline and Fall of the Roman Empire* (1776-1788), lists five causes for the remarkable and rapid growth of Christianity. One of these is 'the miraculous powers of the primitive Church'. He says, 'The Christian Church, from the time of the apostles and their first disciples has claimed an uninterrupted succession of miraculous powers, the gift of tongues, of vision and of prophecy, the power of expelling demons, of healing the sick and of raising the dead.' Gibbon goes on to point out the inconsistency of his own day when 'a latent, and even involuntary, scepticism adheres to the most pious dispositions'. By contrast to the early church, he writes that in the church of his day 'admission of supernatural truths is much less an active consent than a cold and placid acquiescence. Accustomed long since to observe and to respect the invariable order of Nature, our reason, or at least our imagination, is not sufficiently prepared to sustain the visible action of the Deity.' The same could be said even more so of our own day.

HEALING TODAY

God is still healing people today. There are so many wonderful stories of God healing that it is difficult to know which to give as an example. Ajay Gohill told his story at a recent baptism and confirmation service at our church. He was born in Kenya and came to England in 1971. He had been brought up as a Hindu and worked in his family business as a newsagent in Neasden. At the age of twenty-one he contracted erythrodermic psoriasis, a chronic skin disease. His weight dropped from 11.5 to 7.5 stone. He was treated all over the world – in the United States, Germany, Switzerland, Israel and all over England, including Harley Street. He said that he spent 80 per cent of his earnings on trying to find a cure. He took strong drugs which affected his liver. Eventually, he had to give up his job. The disease was all over his body from head to toe. He was so horrible to look at that he could not go swimming or even wear a T-shirt. He lost all his friends. His wife and son left him. He wanted to die. On 20 August 1987 he was in a wheelchair in the Elizabeth Ward of St Thomas' Hospital. He spent over seven weeks in hospital receiving various kinds of treatments. On 14 October he was lying in his bed and wanted to die. He cried out, 'God, if you are watching, let me die – I am sorry if I have done something wrong.' He said that as he prayed he 'felt a presence'. He looked in his locker and pulled out a Good News Bible. He opened it at random and read Psalm 38:

O Lord, don't punish me in your anger! You have wounded me with your arrows; you have struck me down. Because of your anger, I am in great pain; my whole body is diseased because of my sins. I am drowning in the flood of my sins; they are a burden too heavy to bear. Because I have been foolish, my sores stink and rot. I am bowed down, I am crushed; I mourn all day long. I am burning with fever and I am near to death. I am worn out and utterly crushed; my heart is troubled, and I groan with pain. O Lord, you know what I long for; you hear all my groans. My heart is pounding, my strength is gone, and my eyes have lost their brightness. My friends and neighbours will not come near me, because of my sores; even my family keeps away from me. . . . Do not abandon me, O Lord; do not stay away, my God! Help me now, O Lord my saviour! (Psalm 38:1-11, 21-22, GNB).

Each and every verse seemed relevant to him. He prayed for God to heal him and fell into a deep sleep. When he awoke the next morning 'everything looked new'. He went to the bathroom and relaxed in a bath. As he looked at the bathwater, he saw his skin had lifted off and was floating in the bath. He called the nurses in and told them that God was healing him. All his skin was new like a baby's. He had been totally healed. Since then he has been reunited with his son. He says that the inner healing that has taken place in his life is even greater than the physical healing. He says, 'Every day I live for Jesus. I am his servant today.'

God is a God who heals. The Greek word which means 'I save' also means 'I heal'. God is concerned not just about our spiritual salvation, but also about our whole being. One day we shall have a new perfect body but in this life we will never reach perfection. When God heals someone miraculously today we get a glimpse of the future when the final redemption of our bodies will take place (Romans 8:23). Of course not everyone we pray for will necessarily be healed and no human being can ultimately avoid death. Our bodies are decaying. At some point it may even be right to prepare a person for death rather than praying for their healing. Indeed, the

198

love and concern shown to people who are dying, for example, by the hospice movement, gives dignity to the terminally ill and is another outworking of Jesus' commission to care for the sick. So we need to be sensitive to the guidance of the Holy Spirit.

This should not discourage us from praying for people to be healed. The more people we pray for, the more we shall see healed. Those who are not healed usually speak of the blessing of being prayed for – provided they are prayed for with love and sensitivity. I remember a group of us at theological college praying for a man with a bad back. I don't think he was healed, but he said to me afterwards, 'This is the first time since I have been at theological college that I felt anyone cared.' Another man said to me recently that although he had not been healed when he was prayed for, he had had his greatest experience ever of the Spirit of God, and his life has been transformed.

Some are given special gifts of healing (1 Corinthians 12:9). Today, around the world, we find examples of those with an extraordinary gift of healing. This does not mean that we can leave it all to them. The commission to heal is for all of us. Just as we do not all have the gift of evangelism, but we are all called to tell others about Jesus, so we do not all have the gift of healing, but we are all called to pray for the sick.

How in practice do we go about praying for the sick? It is vital to remember that it is God who heals, not us. There is no technique involved. We pray with love and simplicity. The motivation of Jesus was his compassion for people (Mark 1:41; Matthew 9:36). If we love people we will always treat them with respect and dignity. If we believe it is Jesus who heals we will pray with simplicity, because it is not our prayer but the power of God that brings healing.

Here is a simple pattern:

Where does it hurt?

We ask the person who wants prayer for healing what is wrong and what they would like us to pray for.

Why does the person have this condition?

Of course, a leg broken in a car accident will be obvious, but at other times we may need to ask God to show us if there is a root cause to the problem. One woman in our congregation had developed backache with pain in her left hip, which interfered with sleep, movement and work. The doctor prescribed pills for arthritis. She asked for prayer one evening. The girl who was praying for her said that the word 'forgiveness' had come to her mind. After a struggle the woman was able to forgive somebody who had wronged her, and she was partially healed. She was totally healed at the moment she posted a forgiving letter to her friend.

How do I pray?

There are various models in the New Testament which we follow. They are all simple. Sometimes we pray for God to heal in the name of Jesus and we ask the Holy Spirit to come on the person. Prayer may be accompanied by anointing with oil (James 5:14). More often it is accompanied by the laying on of hands (Luke 4:40).

How are they feeling?

After we have prayed we usually ask the person what they are experiencing. Sometimes they feel nothing – in which case we continue to pray. At other times they feel that they are healed, although time alone will tell. On other occasions they feel better but are not totally healed, in which case we continue as Jesus did with the blind man (Mark 8:22-25). We continue praying until we feel it is right to stop.

What next?

After praying for healing it is important to reassure people of God's love for them regardless of whether they are healed or not, and to give them the liberty to come back and be prayed for again. We must avoid putting burdens on people, such as suggesting that it is their lack of faith that has prevented healing from taking place. We always encourage people to go on praying and to ensure that their lives are rooted in the healing community of the church – which is the place where long-term healing so often occurs.

Finally, it is important to persist in praying for people to be healed. It is easy to get discouraged, especially if we do not see immediate dramatic results. We continue because of our obedience to the calling and commission from Jesus Christ to preach the kingdom and to demonstrate its coming by, among other things, healing the sick. If we persist over the years we will see God healing people.

I was once asked to visit a woman in the Brompton Hospital. She was in her thirties, had three children and was pregnant with a fourth. Her common-law husband had left her and she was on her own. Her third child, who was a Down's syndrome child, had a hole in his heart which had been operated on. The operation had not been a success and, not unnaturally, the medical staff wanted to turn the machines off. Three times they asked her if they could turn the machines off and let the baby die. She said no, as she wanted to try one last thing. She wanted someone to pray for him. So I came, and she told me that she didn't believe in God, but she showed me her son. He had tubes all over him and his body was bruised and swollen. She said that the doctors had indicated that even if he recovered he would have brain damage because his heart had stopped for such a long time. She said, 'Will you pray?' So I prayed in the name of Jesus for God to heal him. Then I explained to her how she could give her life to Jesus Christ and she did that. I left, but returned two days later. She came running out the moment she saw me. She said, 'I've been trying to get hold of you: something amazing has happened. The night after you prayed he completely turned the corner. He has recovered.' Within a few days he had gone home. I tried to keep in contact with her, but didn't know where she lived, although she kept leaving messages on the phone. About six months later I was in the lift in another hospital and saw a mother and child whom I did not recognise at once. The woman said, 'Are you Nicky?' I said, 'Yes.' She said, 'That is the little boy you prayed for. It is amazing. Not only has he recovered from the operation, but his hearing, which was bad beforehand, is better. He still has Down's syndrome, but he is much better than he was before.'

Since then I have taken two funerals for other members of that family. At each of them people have come up to me, none of them churchgoers, saying, 'You were the person who prayed for Craig to be healed and God healed him.' They all believe that God healed him, because they know that he was dying. The change in Vivienne, the child's mother, had also made a deep impression on them. She was so changed after coming to Christ that she decided to marry the person with whom she was living. He had come back to her after seeing the change in her life. They are now married and she is totally transformed. On the second occasion, Vivienne went round all the relatives and friends saying, 'I didn't believe, but now I do believe.' Not long afterwards, Craig's uncle and aunt came to church, sat in the front row and gave their lives to Jesus Christ. They did so because they knew they had seen God's power in healing.

14

What about the Church?

Abraham Lincoln once said, 'If all the people who fell asleep in church on Sunday morning were laid out end to end . . . they would be a great deal more comfortable.' Hard pews, unsingable tunes, enforced silence and excruciating boredom are just a few ingredients that make up the common image of church on Sunday. It is seen as an experience through which to grit one's teeth stoically until the aroma of gravy brightens up the prospects of the day. A vicar was taking a small boy around his church and showing him the memorials. 'These are the names of those who died in the Services.' The boy asked, 'Did they die at the morning service or at the evening service?'

Some associate the word 'church' with the clergy. Somebody who is entering the ordained ministry is said to be 'going into the church'. Those embarking on such a career are often viewed with suspicion, and the assumption is made that they are absolutely incapable of doing anything else. Hence a recent advert in the church press: 'Are you forty-five and getting nowhere? Why not consider the Christian ministry?' Clergy are sometimes perceived as: 'Six days invisible, one day incomprehensible!'

Others associate the word 'church' with a particular denomination. For example, Baptists or Methodists. Still others associate the word 'church' with church buildings. They assume that to be a minister you must be interested in church architecture, and when they go on holiday they send their vicar a picture of the local church building. I heard one clergyman imploring his congregation not to send him postcards of churches, telling them he had very little interest in church architecture!

Some tick off 'church' on their list of yearly duties, somewhere between visiting Great Aunt Edna in Hove and making a cake for the village fete. The attitude of others is summed up in a ditty:

> So when I've nothing else to do,
> I think I'll pay a visit,
> So when at last I'm carried in,
> The Lord won't say, 'Who is it?'

There may be an element of truth in some of these views. However, many Christians are seeking to bury this image of the church as it is wholly inadequate when compared to the picture of the church in the New Testament. Many churches are now creating a wonderfully warm and outward-going Christian family which is much closer to the biblical picture. In the New Testament there are over 100 images or analogies of the church, and in this chapter I want to look at five which are central to the understanding of the church.

THE PEOPLE OF GOD

The church is made up of people. The Greek word for church, *ekklesia*, means 'an assembly' or 'gathering of people'. Sometimes the New Testament refers to the universal church (eg, Ephesians 3:10, 21; 5:23, 25, 27, 29, 32). The universal church consists of all those worldwide and down the ages who profess or have professed the name of Christ.

Baptism is a visible mark of being a member of the church. It is also a visible sign of what it means to be a Christian. It signifies cleansing from sin (1 Corinthians 6:11), dying and rising with Christ to a new life (Romans 6:3-5; Colossians 2:12) and the living water which the Holy Spirit brings to our lives (1 Corinthians 12:13). Jesus himself commanded his followers to go and make disciples and to baptise them (Matthew 28:19).

The universal Christian church is vast. According to the *Encyclopaedia Britannica,* it has nearly 1,900,000,000 adherents in 270 countries, consisting of 34 per cent of the world population. In many parts of the world, where there are extreme and oppressive regimes, the church is persecuted. In these parts it is mainly underground but, by all accounts, very strong. In the Third World it is growing rapidly. In some countries, such as Kenya, it is estimated that 80 per cent of the population are now professed Christians. On the other hand, in the free world the church has largely been in decline. According to a survey carried out by *Christian Research,* in the course of the 1990s a million people stopped going to church on an average Sunday in Britain. At one time the West was sending missionaries to the Third World. However, I remember that when I was in Cambridge, three Ugandan missionaries came there to preach the gospel. It struck me then how much the world had changed in the last 150 years and that England needed missionaries as much as anywhere else.

In the New Testament, Paul speaks of local churches, for example the 'Galatian churches' (1 Corinthians 16:1), 'the churches in the province of Asia' (1 Corinthians 16:19) and 'all the churches of Christ' (Romans 16:16). Even those local churches seem at times to have broken down into smaller gatherings which met in homes (Romans 16:5; 1 Corinthians 16:19).

In effect, there seems to have been three types of gathering in the Bible: the large, the medium-sized and the small. These are practical levels at which we experience what the church is: the celebration, congregation and cell. All three are important and complement each other.

The celebration is a large gathering of Christians. This may take place every Sunday in big churches, or when a number of small churches come together for worship. In the Old Testament, the people of God came together for special celebrations with a festive atmosphere at Passover, Pentecost or at the New Year. Today, large gatherings of Christians provide inspiration. Through them many can recapture a vision of the greatness of God and a profound sense of worship. These gatherings of hundreds of Christians together can restore confidence to those who have felt isolated and provide a visible presence of the church in the community. However, on their own such gatherings are not enough. They are not places where Christian friendships can easily develop.

The congregation, in this sense, is a medium-sized gathering. The size makes it possible to know most people and be known by most. It is a place where lasting Christian friendships can be made. It is also a place where the gifts and ministries of the Spirit can be exercised in an atmosphere of love and acceptance, where people are free to risk making mistakes. It is a place where individuals can learn, for example, to give talks, lead worship, pray for the sick, develop the gift of prophecy and learn to pray out loud.

The third level of meeting is the 'cell', which we call the 'small group'. These groups consist of two to twelve people who gather to study the Bible and pray together. It is in these groups that the closest friendships in the church are made. They are characterised by confidentiality (that we can speak openly without fear of gossip), intimacy (that it is a group where we can speak about what really matters in our lives) and accountability (that we are willing to listen to and learn from one another).

THE FAMILY OF GOD

When we receive Jesus Christ into our lives, we become children of God (John 1:12). This is what gives the church its unity. We have God as our Father, Jesus Christ as our Saviour and the Holy Spirit as our indweller. We all belong to one family. Although brothers and sisters may squabble and fall out or not see each other for long periods of time, they still remain brothers and sisters. Nothing can end that relationship. So the church is one, even though it often appears to be divided.

This does not mean that we settle for disunity. Jesus prayed for his followers 'that they may be one' (John 17:11). Paul says, 'Make every effort to keep the unity of the Spirit' (Ephesians 4:3). Like a divided family we should always strive for reconciliation. The incarnation demands a visible expression of our invisible unity. Of course, this unity should not be achieved at the expense of truth but, as the Medieval writer Rupertus Meldenius put it, 'On the necessary points, unity; on the questionable points, liberty; in everything, love.'

At every level we should seek unity – in the small group,

congregation and celebration; within our denomination and between denominations. This unity is brought about as theologians and church leaders get together to debate and work through theological differences. But it is also achieved, often more effectively, by ordinary Christians getting together to worship and work together. The nearer we come to Christ, the nearer we come together. David Watson used a striking illustration. He said:

> When you travel by air and the plane lifts off the ground, the walls and hedges which may seem large and impressive at ground level, at once lose their significance. In the same way, when the power of the Holy Spirit lifts us up together into the conscious realisation of the presence of Jesus, the barriers between us become unimportant. Seated with Christ in the heavenly places, the differences between Christians can often seem petty and marginal.[60]

Since we have the same Father, we are brothers and sisters and are all called to love one another. John puts it very clearly:

> If we say we love God yet hate a brother or sister, we are liars. For any of us who do not love a brother or sister, whom we have seen, cannot love God, whom we have not seen. And he has given us this command: Those who love God must also love one another. Everyone who believes that Jesus is the Christ is born of God, and everyone who loves the father loves his child as well (1 John 4:20 – 5:1).

The Pope's personal preacher, Father Raniero Cantalamessa, addressing a gathering of thousands from many different denominations said, 'When Christians quarrel we say to God: "Choose between us and them." But the Father loves *all* his children. We should say, "We accept as our brothers all those whom you receive as your children."'

We are called to fellowship with one another. The Greek word *koinonia* means 'having in common' or 'sharing'. It is the word used for the marital relationship, the most intimate between human beings. Our fellowship is with God (Father, Son and Holy Spirit – 1 John 1:3; 2 Corinthians 13:14) and with one another (1 John 1:7). Christian fellowship cuts across race, colour, education, background and every other cultural barrier. There is a level of friendship in the church which I have certainly never experienced outside the church.

John Wesley said, 'The New Testament knows nothing of solitary religion.' We are called to fellowship with one another. It is not an optional extra. There are two things we simply cannot do alone. We cannot marry alone and we cannot be a Christian alone. Professor C.E.B. Cranfield put it like this: 'The freelance Christian, who would be a Christian but is too superior to belong to the visible Church upon earth in one of its forms, is simply a contradiction in terms.'

The writer of Hebrews urges his readers, 'Let us consider how we may spur one another on towards love and good deeds. Let us not give up meeting together, as some are in the habit of doing, but let us encourage one another – and all the more as you see the Day approaching' (Hebrews 10:24-25). Often Christians lose their love for the Lord and their enthusiasm for their faith because they neglect fellowship.

One man who found himself in this position was visited by a wise old Christian. They sat in front of the coal fire in the sitting room. The old man never spoke, but went to the coal fire and picked out a red-hot coal with some tongs and put it on the hearth. He still said nothing. In a few minutes the coal had lost its glow. Then he picked it up and put it back in the fire. After a short time it began to glow again. The old man still said nothing at all but, as he got up to leave, the other man knew exactly why he had lost his fervour – a Christian out of fellowship is like a coal out of the fire.

Martin Luther wrote in his diary, 'At home in my house there is no warmth or vigour in one, but in the church when the multitude is gathered together, a fire is kindled in my heart and it breaks its way through.'

THE BODY OF CHRIST

Paul had been persecuting the Christian church when he encountered Jesus Christ on the road to Damascus. Jesus said to him, 'Saul, Saul, why do you persecute *me?*' (Acts 9:4, italics mine). Paul had never met Jesus before so he must have realised that Jesus was saying that, in persecuting Christians, he was persecuting Jesus himself. It may well be that from his encounter Paul realised that the church was, in effect, the body of Christ. 'He calls the church Christ,' wrote the sixteenth-century reformer, Calvin. We Christians are Christ to the world. As the old hymn says:

> He has no hands but our hands
> To do His work today;
> He has no feet but our feet
> To lead men in His way;
> He has no voice but our voice
> To tell men how He died;
> He has no help but our help
> To lead them to His side.

Paul develops this analogy in 1 Corinthians 12. The body is a unit (v. 12), yet this unity does not mean uniformity. 'Those who are members of one another become as diverse as the hand and the ear. That is why the worldlings are so monotonously alike compared with the almost fantastic variety of the saints. Obedience is the road to freedom, humility the road to pleasure, unity the road to personality.'[61] There are 'many parts' and they are all different with 'different kinds of gifts' and 'different kinds of working' (vv. 4-6).

What then should our attitude be to other parts of the body of Christ?

Paul deals with two wrong attitudes. First, he speaks to those who feel inferior and who feel that they have nothing to offer. For example, Paul says the foot may feel inferior to the hand or the ear inferior to the eye (vv. 14-19). It is a human tendency to feel envious of others.

It is easy to look round the church and feel inferior and therefore not needed. As a result we do nothing. In fact we are *all* needed. God has given gifts 'to each one' (v. 7). The term 'to each one' runs through 1 Corinthians 12 as a common thread. Each person has at least one gift which is absolutely necessary for the proper functioning of the body. Unless each of us plays the part God has designed for us, the church will not be able to function as it should. In the following verses, Paul turns to those who feel superior (vv. 21-25) and are saying to others, 'I don't need you.' Again, Paul points out the folly of this position. A body without a foot is not as effective as it might be (see v. 21). Often the parts which are unseen are even more important than those with a higher profile.

The right attitude is one which recognises that we are all in it together. We are all part of a team – each part affects the whole. From Plato onwards, the 'I' has been the personality that gives unity to the body. We do not say, 'My head has an ache.' We say, 'I have a headache.' So it is with the body of Christ. 'If one part suffers, every part suffers with it; if one part is honoured, every part rejoices with it' (v. 26).

Every Christian is a part of the church. John Wimber was once approached by a member of his congregation who had met somebody in great need. After the Sunday service this man told John Wimber of his frustration in trying to get help. 'This man needed a place to stay, food and support while he gets on his feet and looks for a job,' he said. 'I am really frustrated. I tried telephoning the church office, but no one could see me and they couldn't help me. I finally ended up having to let him stay with *me* for the week! Don't you think the church should take care of people like this?' John Wimber says he thought for a moment and then said, 'It looks like *the church* did.'

As we saw in Chapter 8, the problem with the church is that for years it has either been pulpit-centred or altar-centred, according to our different traditions. In both situations the dominant role has been played by the minister or the priest. As Michael Green said, commenting on the spectacular spread of the Pentecostal churches in South America, 'It is . . . due to many causes, but not least to the fact that it is predominantly a lay church.'[62]

A HOLY TEMPLE

The only church building the New Testament speaks about is a building made of people. Paul says that the Christians are 'being built together to become a dwelling in which God lives by his Spirit' (Ephesians 2:22). Jesus is the chief cornerstone. He is the one who founded the church and around whom the church is built. The foundations are 'the apostles and prophets' and the result is a holy temple made of 'living stones'.

In the Old Testament the tabernacle (and later the temple) was central to Israel's worship. This was the place where people went to meet with God. At times his presence filled the temple (1 Kings 8:11) and especially the Holy of Holies. Access to his presence was strictly limited (see Hebrews 9).

Through his death on the cross for us, Jesus opened up access to the Father for all believers all the time. His presence is no longer confined to a physical temple; now he is present by his Spirit with all believers. His presence is especially sensed when Christians gather together (Matthew 18:20). His new temple is the church which is 'a dwelling in which God lives by his Spirit'.

Gordon Fee, Professor of NT at Regent's College, Canada, has written:

> Presence is a delicious word – because it points to one of our truly great gifts. Nothing else can take the place of presence, not gifts, not telephone calls, not pictures, not mementos, nothing. Ask the person who has lost a lifelong mate what they miss the most; the answer is invariably 'presence'. When we are ill, we don't need soothing words nearly as much as we need loved ones to be present. What makes a shared life – games, walks, concerts, outings, and a myriad of other things – so pleasurable? Presence.[63]

The presence of God was what Adam and Eve lost in the Garden of Eden. But God promised that he would restore his presence. In the Old Testament his presence came into the temple. His glory filled the temple. That is why the people of Israel longed to go there. 'How lovely is your dwelling-place, O Lord Almighty! My soul yearns, even faints, for the courts of the Lord; my heart and my flesh cry out for the living God' (Psalm 84:1). One of the reasons the exile was such a disaster is that the people of God were away from God's presence. Then God promised that one day he was going to make his presence more widely known. On the day of Pentecost when the Spirit of God was poured out, the presence of God came to live among his people.

Paul writes of individual Christians, 'Do you not know that your bodies are temples of the Holy Spirit, who is in you, whom you have received from God?' (1 Corinthians 6:19). But more often he writes that the church, the gathered community of Christians, is the temple of the Holy Spirit. That is where God lives by his Spirit.

Under the Old Covenant (before Jesus), access to the Father was through a priest (Hebrews 4:14), who made sacrifices on behalf of believers. Now Jesus, our great high priest, has made the supreme sacrifice of his own life on our behalf. Jesus 'appeared once for all at the end of the ages to do away with sin by the sacrifice of himself' (Hebrews 9:26). We do not need to make further sacrifices for our sins. Rather, we need to be constantly reminded of his sacrifice for us. At the service of Holy Communion, sometimes called the Lord's Supper or the Eucharist, we remember his sacrifice with thanksgiving and partake of its benefits.

As we receive the bread and wine we look in four directions:

We look back with thanks
The bread and wine remind us of the broken body and shed blood of Jesus Christ on the cross. As we receive Communion we look back to the cross with thankfulness that he died for us so that our sins could be forgiven and our guilt removed (Matthew 26:26-28).

We look forward with anticipation
Jesus could have left us some other way to remember his death, but he chose to leave us a meal. A meal is often a way in which we celebrate great occasions. One day in heaven we are going to celebrate for eternity at 'the wedding supper' of Jesus Christ (Revelation 19:9). The bread and wine are a foretaste of this (Luke 22:16; 1 Corinthians 11:26).

We look around at the Christian family
Drinking from one cup and eating the one loaf symbolises our unity in Christ. 'Because there is one loaf, we, who are many, are one body, for we all partake of the one loaf' (1 Corinthians 10:17). That is why we do not receive the bread and the wine on our own. Eating and drinking together in this way should not only remind us of our unity, it should strengthen that unity as we look around at

our brothers and sisters for whom Christ died.

We look up in expectation
The bread and wine represent the body and blood of Jesus. Jesus promised to be with us by his Spirit after his death, and especially wherever Christians meet together: 'Where two or three come together in my name, there am I with them' (Matthew 18:20). So as we receive Communion we look up to Jesus with expectancy. In our experience, we have found that on such occasions there are sometimes conversions, healing and powerful encounters with the presence of Christ.

THE BRIDE OF CHRIST

This is one of the most beautiful analogies of the church in the New Testament. Paul says when speaking of the husband and wife relationship: 'This is a profound mystery – but I am talking about Christ and the church' (Ephesians 5:32). As the Old Testament speaks about God being a husband to Israel (Isaiah 54:1-8), so in the New Testament Paul speaks about Christ being a husband to the church and the model of every human marriage relationship. So he tells husbands to love their wives 'just as Christ loved the church and gave himself up for her to make her holy, cleansing her by the washing with water through the word, and to present her to himself as a radiant church, without stain or wrinkle or any other blemish, but holy and blameless' (Ephesians 5:25-27).

This picture of the holy and radiant church may not accord entirely with the present condition of the church, but we get a glimpse here of what Jesus intends for his church. One day Jesus will return in glory. In the Book of Revelation, John has a vision of the church, 'the new Jerusalem, coming down out of heaven from God, prepared as a bride beautifully dressed for her husband' (Revelation 21:2). Today the church is small and weak. One day we shall see the church as Jesus intends it to be. In the meantime, we must try to bring our experiences as close as possible to the vision of the New Testament.

Our response to Christ's love for us should be one of love for him. The way we show our love for him is by living in holiness and purity – being a bride fit for him and fulfilling his purpose for us. This is his intention for us. This is how his purposes for us will be fulfilled. We are to be changed and to be made beautiful until we are fit to be his bride.

Moreover, his purpose for his church is that we 'may declare the praises of him who called you out of darkness into his wonderful light' (1 Peter 2:9). Declaring his praises involves both worship and witness. Our worship is the expression of our love and reverence for God with our whole beings – heart, mind and bodies. This is the purpose for which we were made. As the Westminster catechism puts it, 'The chief end of man is to glorify God and enjoy him for ever.'

Our witness is our response of love towards other people. He has called us to tell others the good news and draw them into his church – to declare his wonderful deeds to the people around us. In both our worship and our witness we need to find a contemporary expression for eternal truths. God does not change; neither does the gospel. We cannot change our doctrine or our message just to suit passing fashions. But the way in which we worship and the way in which we communicate the gospel must resonate with modern men and women. For many this will mean contemporary music and contemporary language.

If the church was closer to the New Testament images, church services would be far from dull and boring. Indeed, they should be very exciting and sometimes are. The church is made up of the people belonging to God, who are bound together in love as a family with Christ in their midst. They represent Christ to the world, loving their Lord as a bride loves the bridegroom, and being loved by him as a bride is loved by the bridegroom. What a place to be – it should be near heaven on earth.

A young couple who have recently come to faith in Christ wrote:

We have been coming to church for a year now and it already feels like home. The atmosphere of love, friendship and excitement is impossible to find elsewhere. The joy of it far exceeds any evening at a pub, party or restaurant . . . I am shocked to say (although I continue to enjoy all three). Both of us find that Sunday's service and Wednesday's gathering are two high points of the week. At times, it feels like coming up for air, especially as by Wednesday it is easy to be drowning in the deep waters of working life! If we miss either, we feel somehow 'diluted'. Of course, we can keep talking to God together and alone, but I feel that the act of meeting together is the bellows that keep on fanning the flames of our faith.

15

How Can I Make the Most of the Rest of My Life?

W e only get one life. We might wish for more. D. H. Lawrence said, 'If only one could have two lives. The first in which to make one's mistakes . . . and the second in which to profit by them.' But there are no dress rehearsals for life; we are on stage straightaway.

Even if we have made mistakes in the past, it is possible with God's help to make something of what is left. Paul tells us in Romans 12:1-2 how we can do this.

> Therefore, I urge you, brothers and sisters, in view of God's mercy, to offer your bodies as living sacrifices, holy and pleasing to God – which is your spiritual worship. Do not conform any longer to the pattern of this world, but be transformed by the renewing of your mind. Then you will be able to test and approve what God's will is – his good, pleasing and perfect will.

WHAT SHOULD WE DO?

Break with the past

As Christians we are called to be different from the world around us. Paul writes, 'Do not conform any longer to the pattern of this world' (by which he means the world that has shut God out). Or as J. B. Phillips translates this verse, 'Don't let the world around you squeeze you into its own mould'. This is not easy; there is a pressure to conform, to be like everybody else. It is very hard to be different.

A young police officer was taking his final exam at Hendon Police College in north London. Here is one of the questions:

You are on patrol in outer London when an explosion occurs in a gas main in a nearby street. On investigation you find that a large hole has been blown in the footpath and there is an overturned van lying nearby. Inside the van there is a strong smell of alcohol. Both occupants – a man and a woman – are injured. You recognise the woman as the wife of your Divisional Inspector, who is at present away in the USA. A passing motorist stops to offer you assistance and you realise that he is a man who is wanted for armed robbery. Suddenly a man runs out of a nearby house, shouting that his wife is expecting a baby and that the shock of the explosion has made the birth imminent. Another man is crying for help, having been blown into an adjacent canal by the explosion, and he cannot swim.

Bearing in mind the provisions of the Mental Health Act, describe in a few words what actions you would take.

The officer thought for a moment, picked up his pen, and wrote: 'I would take off my uniform and mingle with the crowd.'

We can sympathise with his answer. As a Christian, it is often easier to take off our Christian uniform and 'mingle with the crowd'. But we are called to remain distinctive, to retain our Christian identity, wherever we are and whatever the circumstances.

A Christian is called to be a chrysalis rather than a chameleon. A chrysalis is a pupa which turns into a beautiful butterfly. A chameleon is a lizard with the power to change colour: many can assume shades of green, yellow, cream or dark brown. It is popularly thought to change colour to match its background. Similarly, chameleon Christians merge with their surroundings, happy to be Christians in the company of other Christians, but willing to change their standards in an environment which is not Christian. Legend has it that an experiment was carried out on a chameleon. It was put on a tartan background, could not take the tension, and exploded! The chameleon Christian experiences an almost unbearable tension in his or her life and, unlike the chrysalis Christian, does not reach his or her potential.

Christians are not called to fit in with their background, but to be different. Being different does not mean being odd. We are not called to wear weird clothes or to start speaking in a peculiar religious language. We can be normal! The abnormality that some people feel to be a necessary part of Christianity is complete nonsense. Indeed, a relationship with God through Jesus should bring integration to our personalities. The more like Jesus we become, the more 'normal' we become – in the sense that we become more fully human.

When we follow Christ, we are free to shed patterns and habits that bring us and others down. For example, it means that we should no longer indulge in character assassination behind people's backs. It means we do not need to spend our time grumbling and complaining (if that is what we were like before). It means that we are free not to conform to the world's standards of sexual morality. This might all sound very negative, but it should not be so. Rather than being backbiters, we should be encouragers, constantly looking to build others up out of love for them. Rather than grumbling and complaining, we should be full of thankfulness and joy. Rather than indulging in sexual immorality, we should be demonstrating the blessing of keeping God's standards.

This latter example is one area where Christians are called to be different, but which many find difficult. In my experience of speaking about the Christian faith there is one subject which arises time and time again – the whole question of sexual morality. Questions most frequently asked in this area are, 'What about sex outside marriage? Is it wrong? Where does it say so in the Bible? Why is it wrong?'

God's pattern here, as elsewhere, is far superior to any other. God invented marriage. He also invented sex. He is not, as some seem to think, looking down in astonishment and saying, 'Oh my goodness, whatever will they think of next?' C. S. Lewis pointed out that pleasure is God's idea, not the devil's. The Bible affirms our sexuality. God made us sexual beings and designed our sexual organs for our enjoyment. The Bible celebrates sexual intimacy. In the Song of Songs we see the delight, contentment and satisfaction it brings.

The inventor of sex also tells us how it can be enjoyed to the full. The biblical context of sexual intercourse is the lifelong commitment in marriage between one man and one woman. The Christian doctrine is set out in Genesis 2:24 and quoted by Jesus in Mark 10:7 – 'For this reason a man will leave his father and mother and be united to his wife, and the two will become one flesh.' Marriage involves the public act of leaving parents and making a lifelong commitment. It involves being 'united' with one's partner – the Hebrew word meaning literally 'glued' together – not just physically and biologically, but emotionally, psychologically, spiritually and socially. This is the Christian context of the 'one flesh' union. The biblical doctrine of marriage is the most exciting, thrilling and positive view of marriage that exists. It sets before us God's perfect plan.

God warns of the danger of going outside the boundaries he has laid down. There is no such thing as 'casual sex'. Every act of sexual intercourse effects a 'one flesh' union (1 Corinthians 6:13-20). When this union is broken people get hurt. If you glue two pieces of card together and then pull them apart, you can hear the sound of ripping and see that bits of each are left behind on the other. Similarly, becoming one flesh and then being torn apart leaves scars. We leave broken bits of ourselves in broken relationships. All around us we see what happens when God's standards are ignored. We see broken marriages, broken hearts, hurt children, sexual disease and those whose lives are in a mess. On the other hand, in so many Christian marriages where God's standards are kept, we see the blessing that God intended to bestow on the whole area of sex and marriage. Of course, it is never too late. God's love through Jesus can bring forgiveness, heal scars and restore wholeness to lives that have been torn apart. But it is far better to avoid the necessity of such measures.

So, let us not allow the world to squeeze us into its mould. Let us show the world something far, far better.

Make a new start

Paul says we are to 'be transformed' (Romans 12:2). In other words, we are to be like the chrysalis which changes into a beautiful butterfly. Many are fearful of change in their life: two caterpillars sitting on a leaf saw a butterfly passing by. One turned to the other and said, 'You won't catch me going up in one of those!' Such is our fear of leaving behind what we know.

God does not ask us to leave behind anything that is good. But he does ask us to get rid of the rubbish. Until we leave the rubbish behind we cannot enjoy the wonderful things God has for us. There was a woman who lived on the streets and walked round our parish. She would ask for money and react aggressively to those who refused. She walked the streets for years, accompanied by a mass of plastic bags. When she died, I took the funeral. Although I didn't expect anyone to be there, there were in fact several well-dressed people at the service. I discovered afterwards that this woman had inherited a large fortune. She had acquired a luxurious flat and many valuable paintings, but she chose to live on the streets with her plastic bags full of rubbish. She could not bring herself to leave her lifestyle, and she never enjoyed her inheritance.

As Christians we have inherited far more – all the riches of Christ. In order to enjoy these treasures, we have to leave behind the rubbish in our lives. Paul tells us to 'hate what is evil' (v. 9). That is what must be left behind.

In the verses that follow (Romans 12:9-21) we get a glimpse of some of those treasures to be enjoyed:

> Love must be sincere. Hate what is evil; cling to what is good. Be devoted to one another with mutual affection. Honour one another above yourselves. Never be lacking in zeal, but keep your spiritual fervour, serving the Lord. Be joyful in hope, patient in affliction, faithful in prayer. Share with God's people who are in need. Practise hospitality.

Bless those who persecute you; bless and do not curse. Rejoice with those who rejoice; mourn with those who mourn. Live in harmony with one another. Do not be proud, but be willing to associate with people of low position. Do not be conceited.

Do not repay anyone evil for evil. Be careful to do what is right in the eyes of everybody. If it is possible, as far as it depends on you, live at peace with everyone. Do not take revenge, my friends, but leave room for God's wrath, for it is written: 'It is mine to avenge; I will repay,' says the Lord. On the contrary: 'If your enemies are hungry, feed them; if they are thirsty, give them something to drink. In doing this, you will heap burning coals on their heads.' Do not overcome by evil; but overcome evil with good.

The Greek word for 'sincere' means 'without hypocrisy', or literally 'without play acting' or 'without a mask'. Often, relationships in the world are quite superficial. We all put up fronts to protect ourselves. I certainly did before I was a Christian (and it carried on to some extent afterwards – though it shouldn't have). I said, in effect, 'I don't really like what I am inside, so I will pretend I am somebody different.'

If other people are doing the same then there are two 'fronts' or 'masks' meeting. The real people never meet. This is the opposite of 'sincere love'. Sincere love means taking off our masks and daring to reveal who we are. When we know that God loves us as we are, we are set free to take off our masks. This means that there is a completely new depth in our relationships.

Sometimes people are cynical about enthusiasm, but there is nothing wrong with it. There is a joy and excitement, a 'spiritual fervour' (v. 11) which comes from our relationship with God. This initial experience of Christ is meant to last, and not to peter out. Paul says, '*Never* be lacking in zeal,' but, '*keep* your spiritual fervour, serving the Lord.' The longer we have been Christians, the more enthusiastic we should be.

Paul urges Christians to live in harmony with one another and to be generous (v. 13), hospitable (v. 13), forgiving (v. 14), empathetic (v. 15), and to live at peace with everyone (v. 18). It is a glorious picture of the Christian family into which God calls us, beckoning us into an atmosphere of love, joy, patience, faithfulness, generosity, hospitality, blessing, rejoicing, harmony, humility and peace; where good is not overcome by evil, but evil is overcome by good. These are some of the treasures in store when we leave behind the rubbish.

HOW DO WE DO IT?

'Present your bodies . . .'
This requires an act of the will. Paul commands us, in view of everything that God has done for us, to offer our bodies as living sacrifices, holy and pleasing to God (Romans 12:1). God wants us to offer all of ourselves and all of our lives.

First, we offer our time. Our time is our most valuable possession and we need to give God all of it. This does not mean we spend all of it in prayer and Bible study, but that we allow his priorities to be established in our lives.

It is easy to get our priorities wrong. An advertisement appeared in a newspaper: 'Farmer seeks lady with tractor with view to companionship and possible marriage. Please send picture – of tractor.' I don't think the farmer had his priorities quite right. Our priorities must be our relationships, and our number one priority is our relationship with God. We need to set aside time to be alone with him. We also need to set aside time to be with other Christians – on Sundays and perhaps some mid-week meeting where we can encourage one another.

Secondly, we need to offer our ambitions to the Lord, saying to him, 'Lord, I trust you with my ambitions and hand them over to you.' He asks us to seek his kingdom and his righteousness as our foremost ambition and then he promises to meet all our other needs (Matthew 6:33). This does not necessarily mean that our former ambitions disappear; they may become secondary to Christ's ambitions for us. There is nothing wrong with wanting to be successful in our job, provided that our motivation in everything is seeking his kingdom and his righteousness, and that we use what we have for his glory.

Thirdly, we need to offer him our possessions and our money. In the New Testament there is no ban on private property or making money or saving or even enjoying the good things of life. What is forbidden is a selfish accumulation for ourselves, an unhealthy obsession with material things and putting our trust in riches. What promises security leads to perpetual insecurity and leads us away from God (Matthew 7:9-24). Generous giving is the appropriate response to the generosity of God and the needs of others around us. It is also the best way to break the hold of materialism in our lives.

Next, we need to give him our ears (that is, what we listen to) – to be prepared to stop listening to gossip and other things that drag us and others down. Instead we need to attune our ears to hearing what God is saying to us through the Bible, through prayer and through books and tapes and so on. We offer him our eyes and what we see. Again, some things we look at can harm us through jealousy, lust or some other sin. Other things can lead us closer to God. Rather than criticising the people we meet, we should see them through God's eyes and ask, 'How can I be a blessing to that person?'

Then we need to give him our mouths. The apostle James reminds us what a powerful instrument the tongue is (James 3:1-12). We can use our tongues to destroy, to deceive, to curse, to gossip or to draw attention to ourselves. Or we can use our tongues to worship God and to encourage others. Further, we offer him our hands. We can use our hands either to take for ourselves or to give to others in practical acts of service. Finally, we offer him our sexuality. We can either use our sexuality for our own self-gratification or we can reserve it for the good and pleasure of our marriage partner.

We cannot pick and choose. Paul says, 'Present your bodies' – that is every part of us. The extraordinary paradox is that as we give him everything, we find freedom. Living for ourselves is slavery; but 'his service is perfect freedom' (as the *Book of Common Prayer* puts it).

'. . . as living sacrifices'

There will be a cost to doing all this. It may involve some sacrifice. As the commentator William Barclay put it, 'Jesus came not to make life easy but to make men great.' We have to be prepared to go God's way and not ours. We have to be willing to give up anything in our lives which we know is wrong and put things right where restitution is required, and we need to be willing to fly his flag in a world that may be hostile to the Christian faith.

In many parts of the world, being a Christian involves physical persecution. More Christians have died for their faith in this century than in any other. Others are imprisoned and tortured. We, in the free world, are privileged to live in a society where Christians are not persecuted. The criticism and mocking we may receive are hardly worth mentioning compared to the suffering of the early church and the persecuted church today.

Nevertheless, our faith may involve making sacrifices. For example, I have a friend who was disinherited by his parents when he became a Christian. I know one couple who had to sell their home because they felt that as Christians they must let the Inland Revenue know that over the years they had not been entirely honest in their tax returns.

I had a great friend who was sleeping with his girlfriend before he became a Christian. When he began to look at the Christian faith, he realised that this would have to change if he put his faith in Christ. For many months he wrestled with it. Eventually both he and his girlfriend became Christians and decided that from that moment they would stop sleeping together. For various reasons they were not in a position to get married for another two-and-a-half years. There was a sacrifice involved for them, although they do not see it in that way. God has blessed them richly with a happy marriage and four wonderful children. But at the time there was a cost involved.

WHY SHOULD WE DO IT?

What God has planned for our future

God loves us and wants the very best for our lives. He wants us to entrust our lives to him so that we can 'test and approve what God's will is – his good, pleasing and perfect will' (Romans 12:2).

I sometimes think that the chief work of the devil is to give people a false view of God. The Hebrew word for 'Satan' means 'slanderer'. He slanders God, telling us that he is not to be trusted. He tells us God is a spoilsport and that he wants to ruin our lives.

Often we believe these lies. We think that if we trust our Father in heaven with our lives he will take away all our enjoyment in life. Imagine a human parent like that. Suppose one of my sons were to come to me and say, 'Daddy, I want to give you my day to spend it however you want.' Of course, I would not say, 'Right, that is what I have been waiting for. You can spend the day locked in the cupboard!'

It is absurd even to consider that God would treat us worse than a human parent. He loves us more than any human parent and wants the very best for our lives. His will for us is *good*. He wants the very best (as every good parent does). It is *pleasing* – it will please him and us in the long run. It is *perfect* – we will not be able to improve on it.

Sadly, people feel they can improve on it. They think, 'I can do a little better than God. God is a bit out of touch. He hasn't caught up with the modern world and the things that we enjoy. I think I will run my own life and keep God well out of it.' But we can never do a better job than God, and sometimes we end up making an awful mess.

One of my sons was given some homework that involved making an advertisement for a Roman slave market. It was a school project and he spent most of the weekend doing it. When he had finished the drawing and written all the inscriptions, he wanted to make it look 2,000 years old. The way to do that, he had been told, is to hold the paper over a flame until it goes brown, which gives it the appearance of age. It is quite a tricky job for a nine-year-old, so my wife Pippa offered to help – several times – but could not persuade him. He insisted on doing it himself. The result was that the advertisement was burned to a cinder, accompanied by many tears of frustration and hurt pride.

Some people insist on running their own lives. They do not want any help, they will not trust God, and often it ends in tears. But God gives us a second chance. My son did his poster again and this time he trusted Pippa to do the delicate singeing operation. If we will trust God with our lives, then he will show us what his will is – his good, pleasing and perfect will.

What God has done for us
The little sacrifices he asks us to make are nothing when we compare them with the sacrifice that God made for us. C. T. Studd, the nineteenth-century England cricket captain who gave up wealth and comfort (and cricket!) to serve God in inland China, once said, 'If Jesus Christ be God, and he died for me,

nothing is too hard for me to do for him.' C. T. Studd was looking to Jesus. The writer of Hebrews urges us, 'Let us run with perseverance the race that is set before us, looking to Jesus the pioneer and perfecter of our faith, who for the joy that was set before him endured the cross, despising the shame, and is seated at the right hand of the throne of God' (Hebrews 12:1-2, RSV).

As we look at Jesus, God's only Son who 'endured the cross', we see how much God loves us. It is absurd not to trust him. If God loves us so much we can be sure he will not deprive us of anything good. Paul wrote, 'He who did not spare his own Son, but gave him up for us all – how will he not also, along with him, graciously give us all things?' (Romans 8:32). Our motivation for living the Christian life is the love of the Father. Our model in life is the example of the Son. The means by which we can live this life is the power of the Holy Spirit.

How great God is and what a privilege it is to walk in a relationship with him, to be loved by him and to serve him all our lives. It is the best, most rewarding, fulfilling, meaningful, satisfying way to live. Indeed it is here we find the answers to the great questions of life.

Notes

1. Ronald Brown (ed), *Bishop's Brew* (Arthur James Ltd, 1989).
2. By kind permission of Bernard Levin.
3. *Ibid.*
4. C. S. Lewis, *Timeless at Heart*, Christian Apologetics (Fount).
5. C. S. Lewis, *Surprised by Joy* (Fontana, 1955).
6. John Martyn, *Church of England Newspaper*, 2nd November 1990.
7. Josephus, Antiquities, XVIII 63f. Even if, as some suggest, the text has been corrupted, none the less the evidence of Josephus confirms the historical existence of Jesus.
8. F. J. A. Hort, *The New Testament in the Original Greek*, Vol. I, page 561 (New York: Macmillan Co).
9. Sir Frederic Kenyon, *The Bible and Archaeology* (Harper and Row, 1940).
10. If you are interested in pursuing the subject of gospel historicity, I would recommend reading R. T. France, *The Evidence for Jesus* from *The Jesus Library* (Hodder & Stoughton, 1986) or N.T. Wright, *Jesus and the Victory of God* (SPCK, 1996).
11. C. S. Lewis, *Mere Christianity* (Fount, 1952).
12. *Ibid.*
13. Bernard Ramm, *Protestant Christian Evidence* (Moody Press).

14. By kind permission of Bernard Levin.

15. Lord Hailsham, *The Door Wherein I Went* (Fount/Collins, 1975).

16. Wilbur Smith, *The Incomparable Book* (Beacon Publications, 1961).

17. Josh McDowell, *The Resurrection Factor* (Here's Life Publishers).

18. Michael Green, *Evangelism through the Local Church* (Hodder & Stoughton, 1990).

19. Michael Green, *Man Alive* (InterVarsity Press, 1968).

20. C. S. Lewis, *Surprised by Joy* (Fontana, 1955).

21. Cat.rud.I, 8, 4; PL 40, 319.

22. Bishop J. C. Ryle, *Expository Thoughts on The Gospel*, Vol. III, John 1:1-John 10:30 (Evangelical Press, 1977).

23. *The Journal of the Lawyers' Christian Fellowship.*

24. John Stott, *The Cross of Christ* (IVP, 1996). See also *Catechism of the Catholic Church*, Chapter 2, line 444, paragraph 615, entitled: 'Jesus substitutes his obedience for our disobedience.' By his obedience unto death, Jesus accomplished the substitution of the suffering Servant, who 'makes himself an *offering for sin*', when 'he bore the sin of many', and who 'shall make many to be accounted righteous', for 'he shall bear their iniquities'.

25. Bishop Michael Marshall, *Church of England Newspaper*, 9th August 1991.

26. Father Raneiro Cantalamessa, *Life in the Lordship of Christ* (Sheed & Ward, 1989).

27. We (of course) need to deal with all religious concepts using metaphors and parables. For the atonement there is no one seminal metaphor, no one all-encompassing parable. All are approximations which, like the radii of a circle, converge on the same central point without ever quite touching it.

28. John Wimber, *Equipping the Saints* Vol. 2, No. 2, Spring 1988 (Vineyard Ministries Int.).

29. Lesslie Newbigin, *Foolishness to the Greeks* (SPCK, 1995).

30. C. S. Lewis, *The Last Battle* (HarperCollins, 1956).

31. John Stott, *Christian Counter-Culture* (InterVarsity Press, 1978).

32. Quoted in John Stott, *Christian Counter-Culture* (InterVarsity Press, 1978).

33. John W. Wenham, *Christ and the Bible* (Tyndale: USA, 1972).

34. John Pollock, *Billy Graham: the Authorised Biography* (Hodder & Stoughton, 1966).

35. Bishop Stephen Neill, *The Supremacy of Jesus* (Hodder & Stoughton, 1984).

36. *Family Magazine.*

37. J. I. Packer, *Knowing God* (Hodder & Stoughton, 1973).

38. 'Saints' is the New Testament way of describing all Christians (eg, Philippians 1:1).

39. Michael Bourdeaux, *Risen Indeed* (Darton, Longman & Todd, 1983).

40. John Eddison, *A Study in Spiritual Power* (Highland, 1982).

41. *Ibid.*

42. F. W. Bourne, *Billy Bray: The King's Son* (Epworth Press, 1937).

43. J. Hopkins & H. Richardson (eds.), *Anselm of Canterbury, Proslogion Vol I* (SCM Press, 1974).

44. Malcolm Muggeridge, *Conversion* (Collins, 1988).

45. Richard Wurmbrand, *In God's Underground* (Hodder & Stoughton).

46. Eddie Gibbs, *I Believe in Church Growth* (Hodder & Stoughton).

47. David Watson, *One in the Spirit* (Hodder & Stoughton).

48. Murray Watts, *Rolling in the Aisles* (Monarch Publications, 1987).

49. There has been a great deal of discussion in recent years about whether this experience of the Holy Spirit should be described as 'baptism', 'filling', 'releasing', 'empowering' or some other term. For all that has been said and written on the subject, I do not think it is entirely clear from the New Testament which is the right term. What is clear is that we need the experience of the power of the Holy Spirit in our lives. I myself think that the filling of the Holy Spirit is the most faithful to the New Testament and I have used that expression in this chapter.

50. Martyn Lloyd-Jones, *Romans,* Vol. VIII (Banner of Truth, 1974).

51. Wimber & Springer (eds), *Riding the Third Wave* (Marshall Pickering).

52. Alan MacDonald, *Films in Close Up* (Frameworks, 1991).

53. Michael Green, *I Believe in Satan's Downfall* (Hodder & Stoughton, 1981).

54. Jean-Baptiste Vianney.

55. C. S. Lewis, *The Screwtape Letters* (Fount, 1942).

56. Michael Green, *I Believe in Satan's Downfall* (Hodder & Stoughton, 1981).

57. C. S. Lewis, *The Great Divorce* (Fount, 1973).

58. J. C. Pollock, *Hudson Taylor and Maria* (Hodder & Stoughton, 1962).

59. Irenaeus, *Against Heresies,* II Ch XXXII.

60. David Watson, *I Believe in the Church* (Hodder & Stoughton, 1978).

61. C. S. Lewis, *Fern Seeds and Elephants* (Fontana, 1975).

62. Michael Green, *Called to Serve* (Hodder & Stoughton, 1964). With thanks to the Curtis Brown Agency.

63. Gordon Fee, *Paul, The Spirit and the People of God* (Hodder & Stoughton, 1997).

The Alpha Course

The Alpha Course is a practical introduction to the Christian faith initiated by Holy Trinity Brompton in London, and now being run by thousands of churches, of many denominations, throughout the world.

For more information about Alpha, and related ministries such as The Marriage Course and The Marriage Preparation Course, please see:

alpha.org

Or contact:

Alpha International
Holy Trinity Brompton
Brompton Road
London SW7 1JA
Tel: 0845 644 7544
Email: info@alpha.org

If you would like a copy of the Alpha Publications Brochure, outlining details of resources available for purchase, or to order course materials, please contact the **Alpha Publications Hotline** on:

Tel: 0845 758 1278

To order from overseas:
Tel: +44 1228 611749
Fax: +44 1228 514949

 Kingsway Publications

Alpha

Alpha titles available

Why Jesus?   A booklet – given to all participants at the start of the Alpha course. 'The clearest, best illustrated and most challenging short presentation of Jesus that I know.' – Michael Green

Why Christmas?   The Christmas version of *Why Jesus?*

Searching Issues   The seven issues most often raised by participants on the Alpha course: suffering, other religions, sex before marriage, the New Age, homosexuality, science and Christianity, and the Trinity. Also available as booklets.

A Life Worth Living   What happens after Alpha? Based on the book of Philippians, this is an invaluable next step for those who have just completed the Alpha course, and for anyone eager to put their faith on a firm biblical footing.

Telling Others   The theological principles and the practical details of how courses are run. Each alternate chapter consists of a testimony of someone whose life has been changed by God through an Alpha course.

Challenging Lifestyle   Studies in the Sermon on the Mount showing how Jesus' teaching flies in the face of modern lifestyle and presents us with a radical alternative.

The Heart of Revival   Ten Bible studies based on the book of Isaiah, drawing out important truths for today by interpreting some of the teaching of the Old Testament prophet Isaiah. The book seeks to understand what revival might mean and how we can prepare to be part of it.

30 Days   Nicky Gumbel selects thirty passages from the Old and New Testament which can be read over thirty days. It is designed for those on an Alpha course and others who are interested in beginning to explore the Bible.

*All titles are by Nicky Gumbel, who is vicar of
Holy Trinity Brompton*

—— ❖ ——